Praise for *No Regrets*

"*No Regrets* is . . . destined to take its place alongside the other great self-help guides of our time. Hamilton Beazley is a remarkable writer who has the distinct ability to understand the most complex inner workings of the human spirit and mind. With insight and respect, Beazley compassionately depicts the strategies and tactics that can help others change the architecture of regret to improve virtually every aspect of their being. In his inspired ten-step program, Beazley failed to mention that very first step to having no regrets is to read this book."

—Howard J. Shaffer, Ph.D., Associate Professor and Director,
Division on Addictions, Harvard Medical School

"We spend much of our lives fruitlessly wishing we had made other choices. We somehow believe that when we are not pleased with the consequences of our decisions that an alternative would have been better. The reality is that if we had made another decision we would have had different results. We have no assurances the results would have been better. In *No Regrets,* Hamilton Beazley has provided a truly outstanding process for dealing with our self doubts that result from second guessing our decisions. This is a much-needed process that will help many to accept their human condition in greater comfort."

—Pia Mellody, author of *Facing Codependence,*
Facing Love Addiction, and *The Intimacy Factor*

"A boon to anyone struggling to let go of the heartache caused by regret."

—Susan Anderson, author of *The Journey*
from Abandonment to Healing

"This book is about the dynamics of inner life—anyone's. It brilliantly exposes how people have moved or can move beyond regret to health and vitality."

—The Rt. Rev. Claude E. Payne, D.D.,
Episcopal Bishop of Texas, Retired

"*No Regrets* carries the hopeful message that we can rid ourselves of the regrets that nibble away at our vitality, competence, and joy in the world. Whether the regret is an angry exchange we can't seem to forget or something as shattering as the death of a child, Beazley's ten-step program can release us from bondage into freedom."

—Martha Hickman, author of *Healing After Loss*

NO REGRETS

NO REGRETS

*A Ten-Step Program for
Living in the Present and
Leaving the Past Behind*

HAMILTON BEAZLEY, PH.D.

WILEY

John Wiley & Sons, Inc.

Published by John Wiley & Sons, Inc., Hoboken, New Jersey
Published simultaneously in Canada

For general information about our other products and services, please contact our Customer Care Department within the United States at (800) 762-2974, outside the United States at (317) 572-3993 or fax (317) 572-4002.

Wiley also publishes its books in a variety of electronic formats. Some content that appears in print may not be available in electronic books. For more information about Wiley products, visit our web site at www.wiley.com.

Library of Congress Cataloging-in-Publication Data
Beazley, Hamilton, date.
    No regrets : a ten-step program for living in the present and
leaving the past behind / Hamilton Beazley.
        p.   cm.
    Includes bibliographical references and index.
    ISBN: 978-0-471-21295-9
    1. Regret.   I. Title.
BF575 .R33 B43 2004
158.1—dc22

10   9   8   7   6   5   4   3

To Judith Nowak, whose insights, love,
and laughter on the road less traveled have
made all the difference. For you and that
difference, I will always be grateful.
Deo non fortuna.

Contents

ACKNOWLEDGMENTS

This book is ultimately a collaboration with the many people who shared with me their personal stories of regret and with the scholars and practitioners in psychology, psychiatry, and spirituality whom I consulted in researching it. To each of you who gave so generously of your time, knowledge, and spirit, I am most grateful.

The idea for *No Regrets* was suggested to me by my friend Michael K. Deaver, who also challenged me to write the book. I am appreciative of both the suggestion and the challenge, and for his encouragement during the writing process.

The metaphor of "the road less traveled," which is used throughout the book, originated with Robert Frost in his poem "The Road Not Taken." But the phrase was first, or at least most prominently, applied to psychological and spiritual matters by M. Scott Peck, the author of *The Road Less Traveled*. Dr. Peck's landmark work influenced this book and, before that, had an impact on my own life when it was first published. I am indebted to him for popularizing the phrase and for his marvelous book, which is still one of the best guides I know to living a full, rich, and productive life.

I want to acknowledge my obvious debt to Alcoholics Anonymous and its Twelve Step program of recovery for the concept of the steps. Although the Twelve Steps of Alcoholics Anonymous are not the same as the Ten Steps of letting go of regret (with the exception of making amends), they significantly influenced the general framework of the Ten Steps and contain many of the same spiritual principles. I am especially grateful to AA members who generously shared their time with me, explaining the Twelve Steps and the spiritual principles on which the AA program of recovery is based. Their selflessness in helping me understand the Twelve Steps and their willingness to be of service to me and to each other has been truly inspiring.

I am grateful to Dave Tortorelli, who read an early copy of the manuscript, making invaluable suggestions that greatly improved its readability and clarified its concepts. Eliot Hodges suggested structural and other changes. Andre Delbecq, Ila Ziebell, and my godson Brett Hogan made insightful suggestions that enhanced the quality of the book. To each of you, thanks for your time, effort, and support.

I owe Brett special additional thanks. In a previous book of mine, I borrowed his name for the lead character in the book (with his permission). Although the work was nonfiction, its heart was a fictional narrative that described how the character Brett transformed an organization using certain principles described in the book. Since I failed to thank Brett in the acknowledgments for the use of his name, I am acknowledging that usage now. Obviously it was an expression of great affection. So, thanks, Brett, for allowing me to use your name and, more important, for being the wonderful godson you are.

I would like to express my appreciation to Elizabeth Zack, my acquisitions editor at John Wiley & Sons, who supported the book from the beginning and who shepherded it through the acceptance process. Thanks also to Doris S. Michaels, my literary agent at the Doris S. Michaels Literary Agency, who handled the acquisition. I am very grateful to Lisa Considine, my superb editor at Wiley, who did an outstanding job of analyzing the manuscript, working with me on its revisions, and managing the book's publication. I am indebted to Kimberly Monroe-Hill, who oversaw the production process at Wiley with proficiency and grace. And thanks to Denise L. Nielsen for her conscientious and dedicated work in providing editorial and typing assistance that allowed me to meet the publishing deadlines.

No set of acknowledgments for a book like this would be complete without thanking those who have contributed to my own spiritual journey. In particular, I would like to thank the Right Reverend Claude E. Payne, D.D., Episcopal Bishop of Texas, who was first my rector, then my bishop, and, finally, my close and treasured friend; the Reverend Tom Butler, my spiritual adviser of many years to whom I owe more than I could possibly express; Dave Tortorelli, who has taught me many spiritual lessons by his actions and by the example of his life; Ila Ziebell, whose profound sense of the spiritual sustains and inspires me; Andre Delbecq, who deepened my understanding of, and commitment to, spiritual growth through the simple gift of his presence—and through his patient teaching; John Lobuts Jr., who was my mentor in graduate school and who showed me what real generosity is and how noble the human spirit can be; and many other spiritual pilgrims over the years from whom I have benefited by the gentle touch of their lives.

Finally I want to thank my family members for their support during the research and writing process. My late brother, Herbert Malcolm Beazley (1932–2001), was thrilled with the idea of *No Regrets* although, sadly, he did not live to see its publication. My sister-in-law, Norma Dominy Beazley, has been a steadfast supporter of my writing career, encouraging me in many different ways, all of which are gratefully acknowledged here. My godson Andrew Callaway perused several revisions of the manuscript, each time making invaluable suggestions to improve its pace and enhance its effectiveness. Beyond the literary assistance, however, I am grateful to Andrew for expanding my world of experiences and enriching my life in ways I could not have imagined the first time I held him as his godfather.

And the last person to acknowledge is a little one: my twelve-month-old goddaughter, Parker Hamill Callaway, whose captivating smile continually reminds me that the only time that really counts is the present—and that life is an adventure to be embraced with intense curiosity, endless anticipation, and reckless joy.

NO REGRETS

INTRODUCTION
SOMETHING REMARKABLE IS POSSIBLE

"ONCE UPON A TIME" captures the fairy-tale hope that many of us once had for our lives. As dolls and dragons gave way to dating and driving, the world became more complex, time and events piled up, and the innocence that used to characterize us slipped away. "Once upon a time" gradually dissolved into a different, darker view of our experiences: "If only I had . . ." we would say to ourselves. Sometimes over and over. Or perhaps: "If only I hadn't . . ."

We all have regrets. As we grow older and more fully appreciate the mistakes we have made and the opportunities we have missed, the more there is to regret, at least potentially. Many of us ignore these potential regrets and let the real ones go. But not all of us. Some of us hold onto deep and consuming regrets that burden our lives, cripple our relationships, and hobble our future. They may torment us with the slow drip of remorse or the sudden agony of a memory that springs to life and leaves us cringing. Or they sap our strength with painful memories of what once was or might have been. Intermittent or constant, these regrets tie us to a long-dead past, leaving us guilty or ashamed in the present, unable to touch the joy of life or to regain our own sense of preciousness. On the days when such regrets come back, they suck the life out of us and turn us into the walking wounded, into the near-dead.

Regrets can take many forms: a lost love, squandered assets, years of

1

addiction, a failed career, an illegitimate child given up, an abortion, a public disgrace, children who were not well nurtured, financial ruin, a friend's betrayal, missed career opportunities, an alcoholic parent, inadequate schooling, an extramarital affair, the horrors of war, or any other past event or series of events that continues to have a negative impact on the quality of our lives. Perhaps our regrets cluster around one or two devastating experiences: the sudden death of a child or a bitter divorce. Or perhaps they form a constellation of memories collected over time that stab us repeatedly in our present lives: the pain of an orphaned childhood or the agonies of an abusive father.

For some people, it isn't a simple regret but many regrets that continue to hound them. They regret every major decision they have made, convinced that it was wrong. They can't let go and move on. Even in an affluent society—perhaps especially in an affluent society—many people have deep regrets about their lives, regrets that haunt them and hold them prisoner to a past that is no longer real.

But the same regrets that linger as ghosts from our past can be transformed into guides for the present and mentors for our future. They can serve us rather than torment us, lead us to happiness rather than away from it. They can be answers to our prayers rather than drivers of them. Regrets can be opportunities for spiritual and psychological growth that lead to a greater sense of mastery and joy rather than debilitating memories spawning feelings of hopelessness and grief. We can learn to face the past without fearing it, indulging it, or denying it. We can accept it without regret and move on to a rich and productive life. But how?

Letting Go of Regret

This book describes a practical program of ten steps for moving beyond the past and the regret it holds into the present and the rich life it promises. *No Regrets* is about coming to terms with—and then embracing and, finally, releasing—the regrets of our lives so that they can be used productively for our own growth and for the benefit of others. It doesn't matter whether the regrets are constant or intermittent. It doesn't matter whether they are about something we did (or didn't do) or something someone else or fate did (or didn't do). It doesn't matter whether the regrets are about something from yesterday, last year, or a quarter century ago. No matter what our regret and no matter how painful or devastating it has been, something remarkable is possible. That something remarkable is the gift of freedom: freedom from regret.

Letting go of our regrets does not mean denying them or minimizing them. Rather, it means coming to terms with them, releasing the painful emotions they cause, and ending the distortions they are creating in our lives. When regrets interfere with our happiness, when we are more consumed by the past than enriched by the present, it is time to take stock of our regrets—and what they are costing us.

But we can't change the past.

Or can we?

While we cannot change a past event, we *can* change our reaction to it, our understanding of it, and what we do with it. In other words, *we can change the psychological effect of that past event on our lives.* And when we change the psychological effect of something, it is like changing the thing itself. After all, it is the *psychological effect* that determines how the *event* influences us emotionally in the present. So for all practical purposes, we *can* change the past.

Something remarkable *is* possible. We can make the past work for us rather than against us. Whatever our regret, we can come to terms with it. Whatever our regret, we can learn to use its lessons and its gifts. Whatever our regret, we can let it go.

Ten Steps to Letting Go of Regret

The ten-step program described in this book is based on extensive research, including the psychological literature on regrets, resentments, and their healing; spiritual literature on prayer and meditation, forgiveness, and acceptance; interviews with psychiatrists, members of the clergy, and other experts in psychological and spiritual matters; and the methodology of the Twelve Steps originated by Alcoholics Anonymous and used by dozens of other self-help groups. In the process of writing this book, I have spoken with hundreds of people who have wrestled with burdensome regrets, some of whom overcame them and others who did not. Some of their personal stories are told in the following pages, but of course the name of each person has been changed.

The Ten Steps described in the book use spiritual and therapeutic practices that include visualization, journaling, self-examination, cognitive analysis, affirmations, prayer, meditation, and sharing with others. It is possible to be a spiritual person and to practice spiritual principles without being religious, because spirituality is not necessarily the same as religious belief. While established religious traditions provide a structured way to a deeper faith and greater spirituality, it is possible to begin a spiritual journey with no faith in the God of traditional religions. A willingness to trust in something greater than ourselves, whatever that may be, is helpful at the start but not essential. A willingness to come to believe in something greater than ourselves will speed our journey but again is not essential. Atheists and agnostics, devoted followers of a religious tradition, and those whose sense of the spiritual embraces no specific form of worship will all find that the Ten Steps will work for them. All that is required is willingness. Or a willingness to become willing. And the steps can supply that much willingness.

For some of us, however, willingness is not the primary obstacle to letting go of our regrets. A lack of understanding is. We don't know *how* to let go of our regrets and move on. We don't understand the process involved, the steps we need to take in order to find the freedom we seek. *No Regrets* was written to provide that understanding. It will explain how to open the door to a new life—a life without the regrets that burden you. By understanding what you can do and applying that knowledge to your life, you will come to terms with your regrets—and let them go.

This book will lead you in an orderly fashion through each of the Ten Steps, one step at a time, allowing you to proceed at your own pace. *No Regrets* is an interactive book that asks you to participate in certain structured exercises and activities. It is an encouraging book because encouragement is warranted and needed and because a growing sense of mastery and joy should be part of what you are doing.

The Journey

With this book and a willingness to change, you can embark on a great adventure down a road of wonder. Miracles, love, and healing await you. As you travel this journey of discovery, of letting go, and of spiritual growth, you will not be alone. Unanticipated resources will materialize to assist you. Surprising "coincidences" will happen at the precise moment you need them. New acquaintances and old friends will cross your path at just the right time with just the right words. You will find love, support, and guidance in unexpected places and from unexpected individuals. Powerful forces will be mustered on your behalf. If you give yourself to the work of the Ten Steps, you will be protected and led, and you will experience a sense of joy, freedom, and belonging that you could not have imagined. All of these things are not only possible, they are promises.

I began this book as a project to help a friend find a way to let go of a burdensome regret. As always seems to happen when we set out to help someone else, we are helped most of all. In considering the problem of my friend's regret, I had to come to terms with three big regrets of my own that I had not been able to release, including a death I had never been able to grieve. Each of my regrets clearly met the criterion of a burdensome regret: interference with my enjoyment of the present and with the future I wanted to claim for myself. Yet I didn't know what to do about them in a practical way. I couldn't seem to let them go. In researching and writing *No Regrets,* I found a way to do it. I worked the Ten Steps described in this book on my own regrets, and I have let them go. I am amazed by that. And very grateful.

What I have done, you can do, too.

No Regrets will show you how. It will explain how you can let go of burdensome regrets and how to keep new ones from forming. Beyond that, its Ten Steps will enable you to build a richer and more rewarding life, to reclaim the present for yourself, and to shape the future in accordance with the dreams you have for it.

The road to freedom from regret beckons. Come join me and others who have traveled it. We'll show you the way.

PART I

PREPARATION FOR LETTING GO

1

UNDERSTANDING REGRETS

ROBERT FROST'S POEM "The Road Not Taken" begins with an intriguing question introduced by the memorable phrase: "Two roads diverged in a yellow wood." Which road to take? the poem asks. The narrator chose "the one less traveled by," a choice that "made all the difference." But what if he hadn't taken the road less traveled by? What if he had chosen the road *more* traveled by? That choice, too, would have "made all the difference." But what was the "difference" between the two roads, between the one he took and the one he didn't take? Neither he nor we will ever know, because it was the road not taken.

The road not taken is the source of all regrets. It seduces us with its fantasies of what might have been, limitless possibilities that would have unfolded for us "if only . . ." When we are unhappy, we explore these roads through rich and varied fantasies, creating a world of regret around our hopes and dreams that never came true. In our "if only" daydreams, the roads not taken entice us with their infinite possibilities, poisoning the road we did take or were forced to take and the present in which we live.

Life is filled with many choices—and the uncertainty that inevitably accompanies them. We never know what our choices in life will bring. Sometimes we think we know, but we can never really know—we can only guess. Even after we have made a choice, we cannot know what the other choice would have brought. It's still a guess. Whatever road we took—whether a subtle shift in direction or a major change in destination—the road not taken will always be a mystery to us. We cannot know where it might have led us or to what people or events it might have taken us, for good or for ill. But we can imagine. . . .

While many choices in life are easy, some are difficult. Perhaps we are forced to choose between the city we love or the job we covet. Or we have to decide whether to accept or reject a marriage proposal or to make such a proposal. Other choices are less significant or so they appear at the time we make them. We choose between two movies, for example, but the movie we chose reinforces our desire to change careers, which we then do. What seemed to be an inconsequential decision led to a significant change in the direction of our lives.

Sometimes there is no fork at all in the road—only an abrupt turn that produces a dramatic change in our fortunes and in our lives. We have a heart attack, for example, or develop cancer, and we face difficult medical decisions that we had not anticipated. We don't like any of the options, but we have to choose among them or a choice will be made for us by our indecision and inaction. Casey's sister and brother-in-law were killed in a car accident, leaving her with two young nieces to raise. Casey was single, with a glamorous, exciting, and demanding life that left no time for anything more. Suddenly she faced the prospect of raising two little girls. She felt woefully unprepared to be their mother and dreaded the thought of taking them. But there was no one else to take the children except a stranger, which she couldn't bear. The sudden turn in her life was shocking and unwelcome, bringing deep sadness, great fear, and sweeping change. That it later worked out well for her and the children, bringing great rewards to the trio, did not seem a possibility at the time.

But a more welcome turn in the road is also possible. Charlie had all but given up hope of finding a lover when he encountered a woman giving a cooking demonstration at a department store where he was shopping. They started a conversation about the right way to prepare an omelet. The next thing he knew, he had bought an omelet pan and their conversation had turned to other dishes and then to other possibilities. They started dating and eventually married. In such positive but unexpected twists, we move from what appears to be a dead end to a broad highway and an entirely new destination.

Some choices we create ourselves and call them opportunities. Don endured substantial sacrifices to pay for college and earn a degree in computer science. He worked two jobs, ate all his meals at home, and gave up the chance for any meaningful social life. He put up with the long hours and the exhausting schedule because he wanted an enviable job that would pay well and afford him the status he sought. He wanted more choices.

With some roads, we may have spent days pondering the opportunities and the risks a particular fork offered. We had to answer big questions: Should I have children or not; accept that job offer or settle for what I have; seek a divorce or try to forgive? Which choice would make me happier? What should I do? We may have doubted our final choice even as we made it, hoping only for the best, lost in the uncertainty that characterizes life. Our restricted knowledge of the future deprives us of the certainty that retrospection guarantees. Looking back, it is easy to see where we went "wrong" in some of the choices we made in our relationships, careers, investments, and lives. In hindsight, almost any decision is one that we can later regret to some degree. Because all we have to compare that decision to is the mystery of what might have been and the fantasy we hold of it.

Choices and Expectations

Every decision involves a set of expectations about the future. We may articulate these expectations as predictions or leave them as vague hopes, as much feelings as thoughts. But when we choose a road to travel, we do so on the basis of those expectations. When the expectations aren't realized, we regret the decision. We wish we had done something different. If we don't let go of the regret, we begin to revisit the decision—sometimes in sadness, sometimes in anger, sometimes in despair. Perhaps we revisit it over and over. The choice seems so obvious now! How could we have been so foolish? How could we have been so careless? How could we have been so blind? These repetitive visits to the decision gather steam, and we become increasingly angry at ourselves over what we have done or have not done.

On the other hand, perhaps our regret stems not from our own action or inaction but from something someone else did to us—or didn't do for us. Or from an event over which we had no control. A tree falls on our car. The house is flooded. A fire burns up the garage and the two cars inside. We say to ourselves: "If only I had left earlier." "Why didn't I buy flood insurance?" "I should have checked the wiring." Or we contract a debilitating illness that changes our life.

Whatever the cause of the problem, we begin to regret, and our regretting builds until it spirals out of control. We want so much for it to be different, to be the way we had hoped or dreamed, that we cannot accept what has happened as the way it is. We jump into anger, plunge into sadness, or sink into self-pity. We whine in the hope that someone or something will change it, make it better, or take it away. We complain as if we were children believing that our parents will fix it if only we cry enough. Instead of being empowered, we are victimized by the thought of our regrets. Our anger and despair grow, and the conviction develops that we have messed up our lives beyond correction or that life has messed us up beyond redemption. Nothing, we tell ourselves, can help us now. We are sinking in the quicksand of regret.

We return to our regrets over and over, repeatedly thinking:

- "If only I had . . ."
- "If only she hadn't . . ."
- "Why didn't I? . . ."
- "Things would be different if . . ."
- "I can't believe I didn't . . ."
- "If I had it to do over again . . ."
- "If only I had known . . ."
- "If only I hadn't . . ."
- "I'd give anything if . . ."
- "Why, oh, why didn't? . . ."

When we have these thoughts on a repetitive basis about the same regret or when our regrets are intense and painful, we have identified our burdensome regrets—the regrets we need to let go.

Regretting is the act of revisiting past decisions or events, comparing them to what might have been and wishing they had been different. *When we give those past decisions or events the power to hurt us in the present, we have created burdensome regrets that corrode our lives.* Regretting is a trip to the past for which we pay by losing the present. Regretting takes us from today to yesterday, from what is to what was. It carries us from the present, where we are actors with the power to change our lives, to the past, where we are victims lacking that power, victims of what might have been.

Why is it that we regret? Regrets arise from unfulfilled expectations, from shattered hopes and lost dreams, from failures and tragedies, mistakes and misjudgments. They arise naturally out of life's events and are woven into the fabric of the human experience. Regrets are to be expected as part of being alive. They are inevitable, but they don't have to be burdensome. They can be accepted as part of the unique life we have led. All of us have practice in letting go of regrets—we do it many times a week. But these are usually small regrets and easy to manage. "I shouldn't have ordered dessert." "How could he have forgotten my birthday?" "I shouldn't have bought that sweater." These little regrets bother us only briefly and then we let them go.

But some regrets are bigger, more urgent, and not so easy to release. The stakes are much higher than a few added calories or a forgotten birthday, and the consequences are much more severe. Unlike small regrets, these are difficult to release. They are the regrets that entrap us. We become obsessed with the repercussions of our past actions and with the past and present sadness of their consequences. We board the merry-go-round of regret and ride in endless circles of, "If only I had . . . ," "If only I hadn't . . ."

The older we are, the more potential regrets we have to keep or give up. There are more roads not taken, more years to appreciate what has happened to us, and less time to "correct" our mistakes. We will experience many regrets in a lifetime, always with the same two options: Hold onto them or let them go. That choice is always ours.

Ways of Regretting

Regrets come in many forms, but they can be grouped into seven categories, depending upon the cause of the regret. Some regrets develop from multiple causes and so fall into more than one category. As you read through the categories, match them in your mind to your own regrets. Later you will match them on paper. This process of categorizing regrets is part of a larger process of systematic analysis through which you will gain control over your regrets and reduce their power to hurt you.

The seven categories of regret are:

1. Acts you committed (but wish you hadn't)
2. Acts you didn't commit (but wish you had)
3. Acts others committed (that you wish they hadn't)
4. Acts others didn't commit (that you wish they had)
5. Acts of fate or circumstances
6. Inevitable losses (that you regret)
7. Comparisons (that lead you to regret)

Let's take a look at each.

I. Acts You Committed (But Wish You Hadn't)

Regrets in this category arise from *actions that you took that you wish you hadn't taken.* "I shouldn't have said that" is a common such regret. Usually the misspoken words don't produce long-term effects, except in the case of public figures or in families when the words create lifelong rifts between members. Many other actions in this regret category, however, do produce long-term effects and are complex and difficult to let go. One woman regrets her abortion, for example, while another regrets her illegitimate child. A young man squanders his inheritance on cocaine. Another accidentally causes the death of a friend, while another makes an error in judgment that costs him a leg. A woman steals from her company and gets caught or tells a lie that leads to tragic consequences. A man diagnosed with lung cancer stops smoking but it's too late. These examples are *regrets of commission,* acts people committed that they wish they hadn't.

2. Acts You Didn't Commit (But Wish You Had)

These regrets arise from *actions that you did not take that you wish you had taken.* "I should have called on her birthday" is a regret at the minor end of the spectrum. More serious regrets in this category stem from a failure to act that resulted in grave consequences or lost dreams. A woman neglected her child, who now struggles with abandonment issues. A man loses a parent to a sudden heart attack, leaving him with "I love you" left unsaid. Perhaps a passion for writing fiction was squelched in order to pursue a more stable career, despite an obvious talent and a dream of becoming a great novelist.

Missed opportunities are common in this category of regret. Bob didn't buy Microsoft in the 1980s when he predicted its future rise and had plenty of money to buy it. He played it safe instead, investing in blue chips and watching his portfolio underperform the market even as he spent its principal. Now all he can think about is how rich he would have been today, "If only . . ." "How could I have done that?" he continually asks himself. "How could I have been so stupid?"

Julie struggles in a menial job, barely able to make ends meet, because she has no skills and no education beyond high school. She didn't go to college even though her aunt offered to pay for it. She wanted to see the world, hang out with musicians, drift with the wind, and avoid the tedious life of her parents in their boring factory jobs. Somehow the months turned into years. The men who shared her life grew less reliable, the easy jobs less attractive. Now Julie regrets her lack of education. It would all be different, she tells herself, if only she hadn't turned down her aunt's offer. If only she had gone to college. If only . . .

These examples are *regrets of omission,* acts people did not commit that they wish they had.

3. Acts Others Committed (That You Wish They Hadn't)

Regrets in this category arise from *actions that someone else took in relation to you that you wish they hadn't taken.* You may have played a big role, a minor role, or no role at all in creating these regrets, but their consequences were painful. A thoughtless comment about you falls into this category but is generally easy to dismiss. More serious actions may not be. You were defrauded by your best friend and lost everything. Your spouse cheated on you and then sued for divorce, ending the marriage and your dreams for a stable home that would nurture your children. A stranger rapes you. Your best friend commits suicide. You lose your dream job in a power struggle you did not initiate. Whether the actions of others were deliberate or inadvertent, they still hurt. These regrets are caused by *acts of commission by others.*

4. Acts Others Didn't Commit (That You Wish They Had)

Regrets in this category arise from *actions that others did not take in relation to you that you believe they should have taken.* These regrets often involve someone you know—a member of your family, a friend, or a coworker—but not always. A relatively harmless example, although temporarily painful, is having a spouse forget your anniversary. But there are much more serious examples with potentially devastating long-term consequences. Perhaps your parents didn't teach you self-discipline as a child so that you have had to learn it slowly and painfully as an adult. Perhaps you didn't get the promotion to partner that you had been promised and now have to leave the law firm. Perhaps your parents never told you that you were adopted and you only found out after their deaths—when it was too late to talk to them about it or to find out something about your birth parents.

Sometimes, these acts of *omission* by others can also be categorized as acts of *commission.* For example, a woman rejects a man's request to marry her. He can consider it an act of omission—"she didn't marry me"—and that's how he will probably categorize it. But he can also see it as an act of commission instead—"she rejected me." Either way, it hurts, and whether he classifies the regret as an act of commission or reverses it and classifies it as an act of omission makes no difference. In classifying your own regrets, choose the category that seems more appropriate to you.

5. Acts of Fate or Circumstances

These regrets arise *as the result of fate or life circumstances over which you had no control.* A devastating illness, for example, a physical handicap about which nothing could be done, a childhood of poverty, or the early death of a parent are all circumstances beyond the control of people who are nonetheless deeply affected by them. Accidents also fall into this category. A loved one dies in a plane crash or is killed in a drive-by shooting. These are all acts of fate or circumstances over which you have no control.

6. Inevitable Losses (That You Regret)

Regrets in this category arise from the *inevitable losses that life brings.* These regrets are different from regrets born of events or circumstances perceived as negative, because they are shared by everyone who lives long enough. They include losses associated with growing older and with major life transitions. Inevitable losses characterize every age: childhood, adolescence, young adulthood, middle age, and old age. As they grow older, adolescents, for example, must give up the illusion of omnipotentiality (their ability to become anything in life), not to mention their belief in their invulnerability to harm and their own immortality—quite a price to pay for young adulthood. If they are unwilling to pay this price, however, they are doomed to unhappiness. The loss of omnipotentiality, invulnerability to harm, and immortality on earth are inevitable. How we respond to them is not. The loss of youthful beauty, energy, or dexterity, and the decline in physical ability or stamina are, likewise, merely the inevitable losses of staying alive.

Inevitable losses also include those that arise from *favorable events.* In order to get something, we generally have to give up something. Even though the new may be better than the old, most people still do not like having to give up the old. They would prefer to have both. But life doesn't work that way. Where inevitable losses are concerned, the old and the new are mutually exclusive—one must be given up. This giving up makes the change inherent in inevitable losses painful—even when the change brings significant rewards. Giving up—even to get—is experienced as a loss, a kind of death that has to be grieved, accepted, and let go. Great gains often require great losses. We do not have to like this principle, but it governs our life nonetheless.

Keith, for example, accepted a promotion that he had worked hard to earn, but it required him to move from a town where he had many friends to a city where he had no friends. He liked the job but hated the city in which it was located. Keith regretted taking the promotion and making the move, a regret born of good fortune. He wanted the promotion, but he resented what he had to lose to get it. In fact, he resented even having to make the trade. Keith's focus gradually shifted from the gains of his early promotion to the inevitable losses that accompanied them, and he grew bitter, resentful, and unhappy.

7. Comparisons (That Lead You to Regret)

America is a competitive society that loves its lists and rankings: "The Ten Best-Dressed Women"; "The 50 Most Eligible Bachelors"; "The 100 Best Companies to Work For"; "The 500 Wealthiest People . . ." All of these lists compare the "best" to all the rest. In our success-oriented society, rankings are important, which is why these lists fascinate us. Do you agree that *Citizen Kane* is the best motion picture ever made (traditionally number one) or do you prefer *Casablanca* (traditionally number two)? Do you agree with the choices of the Academy of Motion Picture Arts and Sciences when it honors the best actor, actress, director, and motion picture with its annual Oscars?

When it comes to our own life, we also maintain lists, sometimes consciously, sometimes unconsciously. In these private lists, we rank ourselves in relation to those we know and those we don't know but have heard of or read about. We even create lists in which we rank ourselves in comparison to the selves we had hoped to be but never quite became (or even came close to becoming). Where do you stand in the secret rankings of this internal list? Are you at the top of your list, at the bottom, or somewhere in the middle?

These internalized rankings are a potent source of regrets. In fact they can be among the most painful and debilitating of all regrets. By comparing where you are to where you think you ought to be in relation to your idealized self or in relation to others, you create painful "should haves." "Should haves" arise when you compare what you are to what you *"should have"* been, to what you *"should have"* done, or to what you *"should have"* acquired. Regret-producing comparisons come from "losing out" in the:

- Comparisons that you make between yourself and people you know or have read about.
- Comparisons of your life and accomplishments to the expectations that other people or, in some cases, society itself placed on you.
- Comparisons of your present life to the standards that you set for yourself, the dreams that you once had for yourself, or to the potential that you once possessed.

Comparisons such as these create regrets whenever you make them and find yourself lacking.

Holding onto Regrets

We all experience regrets. They are a natural consequence of being alive. Any action we take can conceivably produce a regret. Likewise, any action we *don't take* can produce a regret. While there is no escape from regrets, there *is* escape from *burdensome* regrets. Regrets themselves are not the problem. *The problem is what we do with the regret.* It's easy to dismiss minor regrets, and we have a lot of practice doing that. "I wish I had gone to the movies after all," we tell ourselves and let this little regret go.

Other regrets are more significant, falling into the "lessons learned" category, but we still let them go. These regrets arise from our own acts of commission or omission and even from those of others. With these regrets, we say to ourselves, "I wish I hadn't done that, but I've learned my lesson. I won't do it again." Or, "He was a terrible boss, but he taught me what not to do as a manager." In such cases, we accept that experience is the best teacher, and we move on. Sometimes the "failures" we regret not only bring us lessons but later work out for the best. For example, someone admits, "I felt like hell when I was fired, but it was the best thing that ever happened to me."

When we consider our mistakes objectively and ponder their lessons, we grow in knowledge and, sometimes, wisdom. If we reject the opportunity to learn from our mistakes, we do not grow and may repeat them. Many of us can admit, "I've learned as much from what I've done wrong as from what I've done right." And so we take the lesson in stride and move on with our lives, continuing to meet the present in all its possibilities.

But some regrets are not easily abandoned. "Why didn't I?" becomes a troubling refrain. Even when we continually revisit a regret, however, we are likely to come to terms with it eventually, accept its lessons, and accommodate ourselves to the reality of what happened. We let time heal us and chalk up the regret to experience. And we let it go.

But not always. When the price we paid for the regret seems too high to accept, we balk at releasing it. We conclude that whatever we have learned or could have learned wasn't enough. Whatever fork in the road we took or were forced down, we didn't like it. The consequences devastated us, and we continue to regret them. We revisit the choices that we made or the circumstances that were forced upon us. Instead of reviewing our regrets to mine their lessons, we return to them over and over to bemoan their consequences, still trying to change the outcome, still trying to have things the way we want them. In so doing, we sink into self-pity and inaction, trapped in an ugly past that we refuse to leave.

Regrets pose a problem for us when we revisit them intensely or repeatedly, wishing that things had been different and blaming ourselves or others that they are not. To harbor a regret means to continue to experience the emotions it generated and to suffer from them long after it was appropriate to have worked through them and let them go. When we harbor a regret, we make it an agonizing destination for our reveries and fantasies. We return to it repeatedly in terrible anger or deep grief or recall it periodically with an intense pain that threatens our sense of wholeness, challenges our worth as a person, and sours our happiness. In such instances the regret is no longer a regret. It has become an intolerable burden.

One way to harbor a regret is to ruminate on it. When applied to cows, to ruminate means to chew a cud. When applied to humans, to ruminate is to ponder the same issue at length, to continue, in a sense, to chew it over and over. Rumination is the psychological term for a repetitive thought pattern. But we do not have to ruminate on our regrets to harbor them. We can still be tormented by them whenever their memory is triggered even if we do not regularly revisit them.

A harbored regret assumes a special status in our lives and serves up a special form of suffering. Harbored regrets carry lies that plunge us into unhappiness: We are incapable of success, unworthy of friendship, or guilty beyond forgiveness. Or they make us angry, defensive, and overreactive to the actions or comments of others. We find ourselves unwilling to forgive, consumed with spasms of hatred or thoughts of revenge that cast their shadows over days that might otherwise be festive and light. Burdensome regrets are dark wellsprings of discontent and blame that restrict our possibilities, curtail our pleasures, and hamper our loving.

We all know people whom we admire, who have successful lives, whose company we enjoy, and yet who feel diminished because of their regrets. We see them as admirable, even enviable people. We would like to be like them. How can they not see how unimportant their real or imagined mistakes are in the context of their whole lives? How can they give so much of themselves now and yet live with so much pain and so little pleasure because of things that happened long ago? As mystified as we might be about them, we have no such mystery about ourselves. *They* have no reason to regret, we tell ourselves, in view of their lives—but we do.

Harbored regrets shift our attention from the reality of what life is to the fantasy of what life might have been—a comparison that cannot be made without feelings of sorrow. If we did not pay such a high price for holding onto our regrets, we might indulge them. But unless our regrets are minor enough to be dismissed with a shrug of the shoulders or a nod to experience, we cannot afford to keep them. And we don't have to keep them. We can let them go. But many of us don't. Why not? If the burden of harbored regrets is so heavy, why do we continue to harbor them?

One of the reasons we hold onto our regrets is that we don't know *how* to let them go. We don't know how to begin the process of eliminating these burdensome memories that have become familiar companions and so part of our lives. We have been told by others to "get over" our regrets, and we have even demanded the same thing of ourselves. But how do we do it? How do we let go of regrets without having a plan that lays out the steps we need to take? Without guidance or a structured means of letting go, most of us can't find our way to freedom from regretting.

There is a second reason for holding onto some of our regrets. They are supported by unrealistic thought patterns that we have never examined or challenged effectively. Believing that we have to be perfect is one such pattern that creates many regrets. Taking on undeserved guilt is another. Sometimes regrets provide a "justification" for our inaction, as when we say that it's too late to change from a hated career to something we really like, and so we don't try. Overcoming these unrealistic thought patterns and their negative effects is part of letting go of our regrets. We'll explore how to do that in Step Three ("Changing Toxic Thought Patterns") in chapter 6.

Letting Go of Regret

When I was deep into my regrets and the shambles they had created in parts of my life, it seemed inconceivable to me that I could let them go. That belief was fueled, in part, by a misunderstanding of what it means to let go of a regret. Letting go does not mean denying the regret or the events that created it. Nor does it mean minimizing the serious effects of the regret on me or others: the pain, the harm, and the fear it caused. Rather, it means coming to terms with the actions and circumstances that created the regret, releasing the painful emotions associated with it, and ending the distortions that the regret is creating for me in the present.

Although I acknowledged the regret and the harm it caused, I came to recognize that I no longer had to be a prisoner of it. I could leave the past where my regret still held sway and step into the present where I could change myself and the circumstances of my life. In the process, I let go of the feelings of anger, shame, guilt, and sadness that surrounded my regrets and that had infected my life. That's what healing is.

The spiritual and psychological tools used in conjunction with the Ten Steps to letting go of regret are designed to bring about such healing. And they work. They will lead you to a new understanding of your regrets and a new perspective on your past that will free you from those regrets. Ultimately, the Ten Steps will lead you to forgiveness—of others and yourself.

The Rewards of Letting Go

When you have harbored regrets for a long time, when you relive them intensely or revisit them frequently, you may find it frightening to contemplate letting them go. Regrets can become such a part of your life that you don't know what it would be like to live without them. You may even fear that their absence would leave an emotional hole that would be difficult to fill. Yet as you work the steps, you will discover that letting go brings many rewards that are far greater than the imagined benefits of harboring the regrets. Some of these rewards are:

- Relief from the pain, anger, shame, and guilt of your regrets
- Escape from the domination that regrets exercise over your life, freeing your thoughts and emotions for more productive purposes
- Recognition of the lessons and gifts that have come from your regrets and how you can use them for your own benefit and the benefit of other people
- Greater acceptance of yourself and others
- A new perspective on your unique life experience and a better appreciation of it
- Increased awareness of your ability to be of service to others
- Greater compassion for those who struggle and have struggled, empathy with those who suffer and have suffered, and love for those who are failing and have failed
- A new sense of being comfortable in the world and being a worthy part of the world

- A commitment to living in the present with all its joys, pain, and possibilities

These rewards may seem remote when you are mired in the pain of your regrets, but they are real nonetheless. They come with the healing of regrets. Healing is possible because you are more capable of growth and deserving of grace than you realize, and because you have at your disposal powerful and transforming steps and spiritual and psychological tools to assist you. Your feelings of helplessness in dealing with your regrets will be converted into a mastery of those regrets, bringing joy, satisfaction, and happiness in greater measure than you can presently imagine.

Something remarkable happens when you invoke spiritual power and apply proven psychological techniques to letting go of your regrets. When your purpose is to heal those regrets and live a more rewarding and productive life, you will be aided in many unanticipated ways. You will be introduced to greater forces—forces that will carry you to the edge of the impossible and to the realm of the miraculous. You will dare to renew your hopes for a richer life and to reclaim longed-for goals that your regrets have denied you. The love affair with life that you once experienced will be rekindled and you will perceive new and startling possibilities that will sweep you from the confines of the past to the lush potential of the present.

The Timing of Letting Go

No Regrets allows you to work the Ten Steps at your own pace, with no set timetable except your own. Proceed in a dedicated manner, working steadily and avoiding procrastination whenever possible. Some procrastination is inevitable but acceptable as long as progress is continuing.

Each of us is different, and each of us has different regrets. For some of us, letting go can be accomplished relatively quickly. An "ah-ha" moment takes place, then another and another, and the pieces of the puzzle fall swiftly together. The way out of our regrets is clear, and our release from regrets can be accomplished with some ease and speed. For others, the process of letting go will require more effort and will take longer, but it will bring the same result. Regardless of the timetable, release from burdensome regrets is virtually assured for those who commit themselves to working the Ten-Step program described in this book.

Your timetable for completing the steps will be determined primarily by the priority you place on letting go of your regrets. If it is a high priority, you will start now and stay with it until you have made peace with the past that holds you. We inevitably spend time on what is important to us. How important is it to you to let go of your regrets? If you are serious about letting go, consider how much time you are willing to spend on the steps. Be realistic but compassionate. You are setting these goals for yourself, not for someone else.

What if you don't meet your timetable? Then you don't meet it. Flexibility is important. Unexpected events may arise that will prevent you from devoting the time to which you are committing now. If so, revise the time estimate as you become more familiar with the process. You may want to increase or decrease it. When you have determined what your time commitment will be, write it on a sheet of paper in the form shown below and insert it in this book as a bookmark. You may set the time commitment in minutes per day or hours per week.

My commitment is to spend _____ minutes per day (or _____ hours per week) reading *No Regrets* and working the Ten Steps. If necessary, I will revise this time commitment as my journey progresses.

_____   _____

Signature   Date

Congratulations. You have begun to let go of your regrets.

2

TEN STEPS TO LETTING GO

THOSE OF US WHO HAVE WRESTLED with burdensome regrets know that the process of letting go is not as simple as people without burdensome regrets make it sound. Some of our family members and friends have encouraged us to let go of our regrets, as if it were easy, not realizing how difficult the task is. We know, however, that the experience of those who have let go of their regrets is so different from ours that they can't appreciate what they are asking us to do. Whatever such people know about letting go of regret, we don't know. They declare, "Forget it and move on with your life," because they've done it a thousand times before. They have no basis in their experience to understand what it is like for us. The difficulty of letting go of our regrets, like the price of holding onto them, is greater for us than they can possibly imagine.

Those of us with burdensome regrets have to learn how to let go. Letting go is a process, not a single event. It is a journey of exploration that takes us down an inner path that we may not have traveled much before. Our regrets will not magically disappear as we walk this path, but they will fade away if we diligently apply the Ten Steps and their spiritual and psychological tools.

Regrets reside in us—in our memories—and so that is where we have to deal with them. Our regrets belong to no one else—only to us. It seems like our regrets belong to everyone involved, but they do not. Our regrets are ours and ours alone to manage—to keep or to let go. Other people who were with us when the regret developed may have their own set of regrets, but they are not ours. What they do with theirs is up to them. What we do with ours is up to us.

The belief that we cannot let go of our regrets keeps some of us from trying. We will never let go of our regrets with that attitude. Why should we? But the belief is false. We *can* let go. When we do not let go, it's because we have made that choice. Instead of saying, "I *can't* let go of this regret," try saying, "I'm not *willing* to let go of this regret." Or even, "I *won't* let go of this regret." To see our own complicity in preserving the regrets that cause us pain may be a hard truth. But it's also good news. If we are responsible for holding onto our regrets, then we can let them go.

The one thing we can definitely change in life is us. When we accept responsibility for holding on to our regrets and shift our perspective from *can't* let go to *won't* let go, we move from helplessness to power. Not knowing *how* to let go is not the same as being unable to let go. Because the *how* is something we can learn. The purpose of the Ten Steps is to teach us how to let go of our regrets. But the steps do even more than that. They walk us through the whole process, step by step.

Start now by saying, "I am letting go of this regret" whenever you think of your regret, and stop repeating the fiction, "I *can't* let go." You *can* let go. Acceptance of that fact is fundamental to letting go of your regrets.

One of the tools that you will use in working the Ten Steps is journaling, which is the process of writing about something in a notebook or on a computer. Journaling is an important part of step work, because writing something down makes it more real and focuses your thinking. Journaling is discussed in the next chapter. Now, however, would be a good time to prepare your journal, because you will use it in this chapter.

Begin by deciding whether your journal will be handwritten, permanently stored on a computer, or printed out from a computer. If it's to be handwritten or printed out, choose a loose-leaf binder or a refillable notebook that can handle additional page insertions and that can accommodate dividers for indexing. You will be adding pages as you go along, and some of them will be inserted in the middle of previous writings.

Regardless of the medium you choose for your journal, find a safe place in which to hide it. Without a safe hiding place, you won't feel free to reveal all the details you need in order to let go of your regrets. If your journal is digital, hide it deep in the computer and secure it with a password, or write it on a disk and keep the disk in a secure place. You must always be confident that only you will ever read your journal.

Once your journal is ready, write the following as your first entry: "It's not that I *can't* let go of my regrets, it's that I haven't. I now accept that I *can* let go of my regrets. I am willing to learn how, and I am willing to let them go."

The Ten-Step Process

The process of going through the Ten Steps and applying their principles to your regrets is called "working" the steps. The Ten Steps are said to be "worked" rather than "taken" or "done" because, well, they involve work. To work a step means to:

- Understand the purpose of the step and its role in letting go of your regrets.
- Take the actions the step recommends, applying its principles to your life and changing your behavior accordingly.

Freedom from regret is achieved through working the Ten Steps. After the first step, each of the remaining steps builds on the one before it, so that the steps should be worked in numerical order. Each step will empower you to work the next step. If you try to work the steps out of order, you will lose the power inherent in their design, and your tasks will be more demanding and more daunting. If you skip a step, the next step will be much more difficult. If you eliminate a step, the whole program may fail. On the other hand, the steps do not have to be worked perfectly. The more thoroughly you work them, however, the greater your healing will be. But even a modest effort that takes you through all the steps will produce results and diminish the painful effect of your regrets. The extent to which you want to let of go of those regrets—reflected in how diligently you work the steps—is your choice to make. The positive results you will experience from progressing through the steps is likely to increase your motivation to work them carefully and completely. And you will find that once you have completed a step, the next step will be easier than you could have imagined before you worked it.

In reading this book, there are two basic approaches. You may choose to read through the entire book first before starting any of the steps. After you have completed the book, you then return to the steps to work them one at a time.

Alternatively, you may choose to read only as far in the book as the step you are working. The advantage of the former approach is that it gives you an overview of the entire step process described in the book. The advantage of the latter approach is that it keeps you focused on the step you are working rather than worrying about the steps to come. Future steps will always appear more difficult until the steps before them have been worked. Pick the approach that seems intuitively right for you.

The Ten Steps are as follows:

1. Listing Regrets
2. Examining Regrets
3. Changing Toxic Thought Patterns
4. Grieving Losses
5. Making Amends
6. Identifying Lessons and Gifts
7. Developing Compassion
8. Forgiving Others
9. Forgiving Ourselves
10. Living Free of Regret

If you look at the Ten Steps as a whole, the process of working them may seem intimidating, if not impossible. If you are suddenly seized with the idea that it's time to take out the garbage, take a deep breath instead. The Ten Steps are not worked as a whole, and that is not the way to view them. They are worked individually, one at a time. It is counterproductive at the beginning of a journey of transformation to jump to the final destination, stare at all the distance in between, and imagine the degree of work required to travel it. Instead, focus on the present step and on the next right thing to do, given where you are in the steps and on your journey. As the steps unfold, each will seem just right for the moment, just what you need, just as you need it. If you take the steps one at a time, you will go from one to the next with surprising momentum and be richly rewarded each time. Success in letting go of regrets is achieved one page at a time, one step at a time, one day at a time.

All that is necessary now is the willingness to begin. And you have already demonstrated that much willingness by buying this book and reading up to this chapter. A complete commitment to letting go of your regrets is not required. Perhaps not even 50.1 percent is necessary, because you will grow in your commitment. Willingness will come over time as the rewards of your early efforts reinforce your desire to move forward, and you become ever more committed to what you are trying to do and ever more pleased with what you are achieving.

At this point, you have only one step to work: the first. Therefore, look only at Step One: listing regrets. It will prepare you for the second step: examining regrets. The second step will prepare you for the third: changing toxic thought patterns. And so on through all the steps. The following chapters will lead you through the Ten Steps, with each chapter devoted to a single step. Step One will identify all the regrets you want to let go. Steps Two through Ten will free you from those regrets. You will find that this book is a complete resource for working the steps. Other books, however, have been written about certain aspects of the process of letting go. These books are listed in appendix A, "Recommended Reading," and are worth examining as well.

Overcoming Excuses

"I would let go of my regrets except that . . ." We tend to resist change that takes effort and that raises our fear level, even if the change will benefit us in the long run. This natural reluctance to change often expresses itself in the excuses we offer ourselves or others for holding onto our regrets. Although these excuses may feel like reasons, they are not. Reasons are valid explanations of why we don't want to do something. Excuses are self-serving justifications for why we don't want to do something. Excuses are meant to sound real, but they do not reflect the actual motive. For example, a person might decline a party invitation by saying that he doesn't feel well when, in fact, he doesn't like the host. The dislike of the host is the reason. Not feeling well is the excuse.

When people give a reason for not doing something we have asked them to do, we don't always believe them. Sometimes we decide that their "reason" is an excuse and treat it as such. But when we are dealing with ourselves, we are likely to believe our own excuses, accepting them as if they were reasons. Hence our journey of letting go begins with an examination of various excuses for holding onto regrets.

Some common excuses are described in the following paragraphs. They are reasons only in the imagination, because they have no validity. Ask yourself whether any of these excuses apply to you and your regrets:

1. *"It's too late to let go of my regret."* The assumption behind this excuse is that letting go of regret is a function of time. But the passage of time neither improves nor impairs our ability to let go of regrets. Letting go is a function of willingness—the willingness to look at ourselves and to take certain actions—not a function of time. Whether a regret is old or new has no effect on our ability to let it go. The Ten Steps can be applied to any regret of any age with the same positive result.

2. *"I can't possibly go back and relive all that again."* This excuse sounds like a good reason, but it isn't because of two fatal flaws. The first is that we are already reliving the regret through our refusal to let it go. We do not escape pain by holding onto our regrets. We prolong it. Ironically, the only way to avoid continuously reliving the regret is to relive it but in an organized, purposeful, and supported way so that we can release its pain and let it go. It is true that the trip back may be painful, but the pain will be short lived in comparison to the ongoing pain of holding onto the regret.

   The second flaw in the excuse is its implication that you do not have the strength or courage to do the work of the steps. You do. The strength and courage you need to let go of your regrets will come from working the Ten Steps and using their spiritual and psychological tools. You will be given all the strength you need *as you need it.* What you cannot anticipate at the beginning of the steps is how much you will be assisted along the way by unexpected forces. Various recovery groups attest to this phenomenon. Perhaps it results from the actions taken in working the steps or from applying their spiritual and psychological tools. Perhaps it results from synchronicity, the appearance of meaningful coincidences that provide needed insights, a concept developed by Carl Jung, one of the founders of psychoanalysis. Perhaps it is because the steps make you more open to being helped and more willing and more likely to seek help. Whatever the cause, the result will be a transformed landscape through which to make your journey.

New friends will appear just as you need their counsel, old friends may reappear, and new sources of support will emerge that you could not have imagined when you first began. Coincidences will lead to new insights, unexpected people will encourage you, and events will offer new opportunities for growth and development. Something remarkable happens when you commit to letting go of your regrets and working the Ten Steps.

3. *"I cannot forgive what was done to me"* or *"I could never forgive myself for what I did."* The flaw in both of these excuses is the suggestion that we can't forgive, because something about forgiveness is somehow beyond our control. Forgiveness is never beyond our control. When we refuse to forgive ourselves or others, it is because we *will not* rather than because we *cannot.* Forgiveness is not a function of personal capacity but of willingness. We can forgive ourselves for virtually anything, just as we can forgive other people for virtually anything. The power to forgive is always ours. Forgiveness in cases of great harm may not come easily, and it may not come quickly, but it will come if we work toward it.

This excuse of being unable to forgive may have temporary validity for those of us who don't know *how* to forgive. Perhaps we were not taught as children, have little experience with forgiveness, and have virtually no understanding of it. In such cases, it *is* difficult for us to forgive. But the Ten Steps will teach us how to forgive as well as lead us to that forgiveness. So the excuse is still an excuse—a temporary impediment to letting go of our regrets that will be eliminated through the work of the steps. Forgiveness takes place in the realm of the spiritual, where anything is possible.

4. *"I could never be forgiven for what I did."* This excuse is based on a misunderstanding of what forgiveness is. Forgiveness is not something others do for us. It is something we do for ourselves, and it does not depend upon those we have harmed to be valid. Regardless of the seriousness of our regrets, real forgiveness is always ours to have. A wronged party who does not forgive us after all appropriate amends have been made has a problem, which is not our responsibility to solve. We can be forgiven anyway.

5. *"I will never forget what was done to me."* Letting go of a regret has nothing to do with forgetting that regret or the events that surrounded it. Even after we have let go of a regret, we will still remember it, perhaps for a lifetime. The difference is that the regret will no longer have the power to hurt us, even if it is remembered. So if the phrase is taken literally, we don't have to worry about never forgetting what happened to us. On the other hand, if it is used to mean never forgiving what was done to us, we have already dealt with that excuse.

6. *"I could never forget what I did."* Letting go of a regret does not mean forgetting what we did. It means revisiting the regret in a structured way so that we can work through its pain and eliminate its power to hurt us. We don't forget our regrets, but we do let them go, even when we are the ones who caused them. This excuse is sometimes used to mean "I could never forgive what I did," in which the word "forget" is substituted for "forgive." When the excuse is used with that meaning, it is equally invalid for reasons we have already discussed.

7. *"If I go back to examine the past, I'll get stuck there."* This excuse sounds plausible, but it is not. The opposite is true. It is an *unexamined* past that traps us. An examined past frees us. By using the Ten Steps to analyze our regrets in a structured way and to release them, we find the

freedom from regrets that we seek. Through the steps, we return to the past to let it go, not to wallow in it.

8. *"Now is not the right time."* This excuse is common among those looking for the perfect time to begin something, as though no project should ever be attempted until the stars have lined up completely in its favor. Most projects are started under less than perfect conditions. The ideal time to start is now, regardless. There are some exceptions (immediately after the funeral of a loved one, for example, is probably not the best time to begin examining regrets related to that person), but now is almost always better than later. Too often, later turns into never.

9. *More excuses.* These excuses may not have included all the ones you use for holding onto your regrets. Note in your journal any additional excuses that you have used to keep from letting them go. If some of these excuses appear to be real reasons rather than excuses you can refute, do not be concerned. Write them down and move on. You will deal with them later.

Relating to Yourself

As you embark on the journey of letting go, part of your task will be to relate to yourself in a different way. Just as there are many ways to treat other people, there are many ways to treat yourself. In dealing with yourself, for example, you can be hateful or supportive, encouraging or discouraging, loving or sarcastic, tolerant or judgmental. The way you relate to yourself and others can be described in terms of analogies: as a best friend, a respected colleague, a beloved sibling, a cruel taskmaster, an angry boss. What you say to yourself in your thoughts will differ dramatically depending upon the nature of the relationship you have with yourself.

As you work the Ten Steps, make a conscious and deliberate effort to relate more positively toward yourself. Instead of treating yourself as a failure, a bad person, or someone undeserving of happiness, strive to nurture yourself as if you were your best friend, a favorite sibling, or a beloved child. This shift in mind-set may be new and slow in coming. But it is important.

Pause to consider how you relate to yourself in dealing with your regrets. Are you attacking and blaming rather than loving and supportive? Are you quick to criticize or curse yourself for what you've done in the distant past or seconds before? Are you impatient, intolerant, and unforgiving of yourself? If you behave toward yourself as a sarcastic bully, you are in a difficult position, because living with a bully is exhausting and stress-filled. Do you have a severe, contemptuous attitude toward yourself and your regrets, as in, "Get over it!" Or do you take a different tack and regard yourself as a victim, wallowing in the pain and hopelessness of the past, condemned to suffer for the rest of your life? Or do you alternate between these extremes?

In your journal, summarize how you currently treat yourself regarding your regrets. Use adverbs (cruelly, lovingly, contemptuously) and analogies (like a good friend, a stupid child, a perpetual loser) to describe your relationship with yourself when your thoughts turn to your regrets.

If you relate to yourself in an attacking, self-destructive manner, are you willing to make a commitment to change that way of relating to yourself? If so, describe in your journal how you will treat yourself from now on in dealing with your regrets. Begin by using adverbs. For example: I will treat myself lovingly, patiently, sympathetically, and compassionately.

Now use analogies to describe how you will treat yourself. For example, I will treat myself like a caring older brother, a loving friend, a patient teacher.

Courage

Courage is not the *absence* of fear—it is the overcoming of fear. Courageous people, like cowardly people, are fearful, but they don't give into their fear. They summon their spiritual and psychological resources and conquer it. The difference between the brave and the cowardly is not the presence of fear, but their response to it.

Courageous people understand that excessive fear is an impediment to growth and happiness and that it can be overcome through spiritual resources and the support of others. As you undertake the Ten Steps to letting go of regret, remember that you are a courageous person, whether you yet realize it. All the courage you need will be made available to you as you work the steps. That courage will come from many sources, including the Ten Steps and the spiritual and psychological tools that you will use to assist you in working them. These tools, how they are applied, and what they can do for you are discussed in the next chapter.

3

USING SPIRITUAL AND
PSYCHOLOGICAL TOOLS

IN COMBINATION with the Ten Steps, the spiritual and psychological tools described in this chapter will provide you with the means you need to let go of your regrets. These tools draw upon three types of resources available to all of us as human beings: intellectual, psychological, and spiritual. Our intellectual or mental resources allow us to analyze ideas and events in a logical, rational way in order to determine cause and effect and to make sense of the world. Psychological resources enable us to marshal our intellect and our emotions to change the way we think and feel about ourselves, about others, and about events. Spiritual resources summon powers greater than ourselves to help us do what we cannot do alone.

Each of the spiritual and psychological tools is effective, but each serves a different purpose. Only two of the tools are mandatory: journaling and thought analysis. The others are optional, and whether you choose to apply them to a given step will depend on whether you need them to complete that step. If you encounter resistance to working the steps, more tools will be called for as a means of helping you overcome that resistance. The spiritual and psychological tools and some of their purposes are:

- *Thought analysis:* to analyze your regrets, the events associated with them, the feelings you have about them, and the way in which you think about them; to change the way you think and feel about your regrets.

- *Journaling:* to catalogue and analyze your regrets, to clarify your thoughts about them, and to express your feelings.
- *Prayer:* to gain the insight, courage, discipline, strength, and other resources you need to work each step.
- *Sharing with others:* to gain insight and emotional support from others in working the steps.
- *Affirmations:* to overcome resistance and to facilitate your working the steps.
- *Creative visualization:* to overcome resistance and to facilitate your working the steps.

Thought Analysis

We are in constant conversation with ourselves. We are always silently observing, commenting, challenging, criticizing, joking, or debating with ourselves. This constant internal chatter isn't surprising really. After all, *that's how we think.* I once asked a psychiatrist friend of mine if it meant you were crazy to talk to yourself out loud. "Not at all," she replied, "but it's not very private." Most of us don't expose the committee of voices in our head to the general public; we keep them to ourselves. But we don't necessarily pay much attention to what we're saying to ourselves, either. Oh, we're listening, but we're not listening with a critical, challenging ear. Unless, of course, we're trying to make a decision. Then we have a serious debate with ourselves, and we listen intently as we weigh the pros and cons of our actions, trying to decide.

Thought analysis is a process through which we analyze what we are saying to ourselves about ourselves and others to determine its validity. The goal of thought analysis is to become aware of what we are thinking and expose those thoughts to critical analysis. When we tell ourselves something concerning our regrets that isn't true, isn't realistic, or isn't warranted, we reject the thought, replacing it with a more accurate thought.

As a child, Patty was molested by her father's best friend for two years before she finally found the courage to tell her parents. When the revelation destroyed her father's relationship with the man and sent him to jail,

Patty felt guilty and responsible for what had happened. When the thought recurs that she should have resisted the trusted adult's advances, she now rejects it. Instead, she reminds herself that she was not responsible as a child for what happened to her and that none of it was her fault. The more we practice thought analysis, the more we will learn to act as our own advocate and best friend. We can protect ourselves from unrealistic or unwarranted thoughts and from the negative aspects of our personality that would force us to suffer for the past.

When you truly listen to yourself through thought analysis, you will overhear fascinating conversations. Some of them will contain statements about you or your regrets that you have long accepted as true but that are false. Your favorite false statements will continue to reappear, but they can be rejected by taking three simple steps:

1. Listen critically to every thought that pertains to your regrets.
2. Analyze the validity of each thought by asking yourself such questions as, "Is this statement true?" "Is it fair?" "Is it realistic?"
3. Act on your analysis by rejecting the thought if it is invalid (unfair, untrue, or unrealistic).

This is thought analysis.

For example, repetitive lies like, "You always screw up," "It's all your fault," and "You should have known that was going to happen" can be challenged when you listen critically to what you are saying to yourself. They are challenged by asking yourself if such statements are true. They are not. The truth is that neither you nor anybody else "*always* screws up." Sometimes you get it right. Likewise, it is seldom "all" your fault, although you may have been the major cause of a problem. And since no one can see the future, you should *not* have "known" what was going to happen unless it was highly predictable, and even then, things may not have turned out as foreseen.

Although the process of thought analysis may feel strange at first, the more you practice it, the more it will become second nature to you. In fact, after a while, it will seem odd that you haven't practiced it for a lifetime.

Journaling

A journal is a written record of thoughts, events, reflections, fears, feelings, or anything else worthy of recording that is kept on a regular or even irregular basis. Journals have been around for thousands of years. St. Augustine's *Confessions* from A.D. 396 is a journal of his life. The Victorians (both men and women) raised journal-keeping to a fine art, recording their thoughts in expensive volumes of handcrafted leather.

The purpose of *journaling* in working the steps is to analyze your regrets, organize your thoughts, clarify your emotions, and increase your objectivity. Whenever we reduce something to writing, we shrink it, make it more manageable, and begin to exercise control over it. When we are writing about things that disturb us, this kind of limitation on our imagination is therapeutic, because it puts our situation into perspective and reduces the fear our imagination creates. Journaling is a healing activity. Medical studies have shown that patients with asthma and rheumatoid arthritis who journal daily experience a marked reduction in symptoms.

Journaling exercises are an important part of Ten-Step work. Because our journal will be safely hidden, we can be completely honest in analyzing our regrets, revealing our deepest secrets, greatest fears, and innermost thoughts without the risk of judgment or condemnation. When something angers us, we can vent safely to the journal. When something frightens us, we can confide it to the journal. We can journal about our resistance to the step and about anything else that makes the step difficult to work or that would make working the step easier. Whether we're writing about the present, the past, or the future, our journal helps us carry the burden. And it's always available.

Journaling is largely intuitive, but for newcomers, a few suggestions may make the process more comfortable and more productive:

- *Write freely and without censorship, being as honest and thorough as you can.* Honesty is essential if you are to process your feelings effectively, but it is also essential to productive thought analysis. If you are to be sure that your thoughts are valid and your feelings are in proportion, you must be honest with yourself. If you want to let go of your regrets, you must not kid yourself about those regrets or about your life. Write in the journal honestly and without reservation. Psychological research confirms that when you write freely and without self-censorship, putting your thoughts on paper as they come to you without judging them or editing them for content or grammar, you will tap deep insights, feelings, and beliefs. With a journal, you can write openly, honestly, and without fear. The journal neither judges nor breaks a confidence. What you reveal is safe.

- *Ignore the quality of the writing.* Journal entries do not have to be well written. You do not even have to write in complete sentences, and you can always go back later and change something if you want. A journal is not a literary piece but a working document to help you achieve your goals. Write what you feel the need to write, and write as much and for as long as you want.
- *Be patient.* With practice, journaling will become easier and will seem more natural, even for those who are not natural writers.

Expository writing is the primary means through which a Ten-Step journal is created in letting go of regrets, as in the listing of regrets. Sometimes, however, other forms of writing can be an important supplement to the basic journal, especially when describing or dealing with emotions. Poetry, song lyrics, and short stories can often convey greater emotion than an essaylike paragraph and may be easier for some people to write. Poetry, lyrics, and stories of others can be attached or copied to the journal when they are relevant. In fact, writing itself can be supplemented by other forms of journaling. Depending upon your particular talent, you may prefer to draw in your journal, to paint, or even to paste images cut from magazines and newspapers that represent what you are feeling, what you have lost, or what you had dreamed of having.

Prayer

As far as we know, the idea of God and, hence, of spirituality is as old as humankind. No civilization of which we have any knowledge was without some set of religious beliefs. Religion and spirituality are not the same, however. It is possible to be spiritual without being religious. Although spirituality, like religion, deals with transcendent forces, it does not require a set of specific beliefs, an organized structure, or a corps of religious professionals. *Spirituality does, however, require a faith relationship with something greater than ourselves, something beyond and independent of the material universe (that is, something transcendent).* Generally, that "something" is God, however the individual chooses to define God. The spiritual aspects of the Ten Steps (as opposed to the psychological) are more effective with a faith relationship.

However, the Ten Steps do not define the nature of that faith relationship nor do they define God. A spiritual ground rule of the Ten Steps is that no specific concept of God is required in order to work them or to use their spiritual and psychological tools. For that matter, it isn't necessary to believe in God at all to work the steps. All that is suggested is an *openness* to the existence of some power, force, or principle greater than yourself. You may use whatever term you wish to refer to that power. Traditional terms used to refer to God have included Supreme Being, the Creator, deity, divinity, divine principle, the Great Spirit, higher power, universal mind, the Absolute, the One, a power greater than ourselves, and dozens of other phrases that human beings have used to identify God in hundreds of cultures for thousands of years. This book uses "power greater than ourselves," "higher power," or "God." No definition is offered, however, other than "beyond and independent of the material world."

An openness to some form of spirituality is important in working the Ten Steps, because spiritual tools such as prayer are powerful aids in letting go of our regrets. Prayer allows us to access a power greater than ourselves to help us do what we cannot do on the basis of our own resources. Through prayer, we can overcome resistance, conquer fear, and gain new insights. We will be led to people, events, and circumstances with the power to transform us and to help us achieve our goal of living without regrets. If the spiritual tools are eliminated, leaving only the psychological tools, the possibility of being healed is diminished. Yet what one prays to in working the steps is determined by each individual.

For some people, engaging in prayer is easy and automatic. For others, it is intimidating and awkward. For those who are new to praying, the act can seem an awesome, even fearful, task. Prayer is, after all, an attempt to communicate with God. It raises many questions: "How would I start?" "What words should I use?" Fortunately, the answers are quite simple, and prayer itself is not at all intimidating once you understand it. In fact, prayer is very reassuring. While there are many definitions of prayer, all of them contain the central idea of prayer as words, thoughts, or feelings addressed to a higher power, however defined.

The Meaning of Prayer

There are many possible definitions of prayer. Some of the definitions that might be helpful in understanding prayer are the following:

- Prayer is opening our minds and hearts to God.
- Prayer is a conversation with God in which we have the opportunity to speak and the obligation to listen.
- Prayer is communing with our higher power.
- Prayer is asking to know God's will for us and for the strength and courage to carry it out.
- Prayer is asking God for help and then being open to letting God help us.
- Prayer is acknowledging our needs and then asking God to meet those needs in whatever way God thinks is best.
- Prayer is asking our higher power to heal us and then being willing to be part of that healing.
- Prayer is a recognition of our helplessness and of God's power.
- Prayer is loving attentiveness to the higher power.
- Prayer is making ourselves teachable so that we can learn God's will for us.

Traditional religions have identified five types of prayer according to the purpose of the prayer. A single prayer can fulfill one or more of these purposes:

1. *Petition:* Prayers of petition contain a request for ourselves and are the most common type of prayer. They come quite naturally to most of us and include requests for healing, safety, and other assistance of whatever kind. The simplest form of petition is, "God, help me."

2. *Intercession:* In prayers of intercession, we intercede or speak on behalf of others, asking that something be done for their benefit. Such prayers are often said for family, friends, coworkers, and others who are important to us, but they may also be said for acquaintances, strangers, those whom we have hurt, those who have hurt us, and those whom we dislike or hate. A simple form of intercession would be, "Please protect my baby."

3. *Confession:* This prayer is an admission of having done something wrong. It generally includes an expression of sorrow, a request for the strength and courage to make the amends we need to make, an appeal for forgiveness, and the power to avoid repeating the behavior. A simple confession would be, "Please forgive me for what I've done. Grant me the strength and courage to make amends, and help me to do the right thing in the future."

4. *Thanksgiving:* This prayer expresses gratitude for God's presence in our lives, for the blessings we have received, the spiritual and material gifts we have been given, and the protection God has afforded us. Prayers of thanksgiving support our humility because they acknowledge our debt to God for all that we have. A simple prayer of thanksgiving would be, "Thank you for all my blessings, especially for my loving family, my good health, and the food I eat."

5. *Adoration:* The most difficult to describe of the five types of prayer, adoration is an appreciation of the power, love, majesty, and wonder of God. Sunrises and sunsets, music, paintings, and other works of art sometimes elicit a sense of adoration as we marvel at the beauty and the exquisiteness of life and nature. Adoration is an experience of the awesome power of God and is a natural expression of our gratitude and wonder at the power of the divine. Prayers of adoration are more often felt than said.

In saying a prayer with all five components, we would acknowledge our sense of the power, wonder, and love of God; confess our mistakes and ask forgiveness; pray for others; petition God to meet our own needs; and thank God for all the blessings we have received. But not every prayer is so complete, nor does it have to be. We may, for example, pray spontaneously in response to events that confront us. We might ask God to help us in a difficult situation, thank God for saving us from harm in a close call, rejoice at the unexpected beauty around us, or pray urgently for the health of a friend.

To pray when we are in trouble or in need is to go to God in a state of helplessness, talk about our pain and distress, and ask for God's assistance. To pray is not to beg for help, however, but merely to ask for it. To pray is also to go to God in times of joy. The logic of prayer is irrefutable when we feel helpless, cornered, and desperate. We speak the words, "God, help me" almost without thinking. Yet we resist prayer when our pain is less intense. In doing so, we miss an opportunity to seek God's assistance with our daily difficulties when a greater wisdom than our own is needed. Daily prayer establishes regular communication with God, which makes prayer easier in both the good and the bad times, bringing us spiritual gifts we would not otherwise have received.

We naturally associate prayer with people of faith, but what if we have little faith and still want to pray? What do we do then? We pray. What if we have no faith and still want to pray? We pray. That is the beauty of prayer. Our willingness to pray is a form of faith. "God, help me," the pained cry of the hurting heart, is an act of faith that always brings a response. That response may or may not be the one we wanted or expected, and it may not be within the time frame we demanded. But whatever the response, it will be the best possible answer to our need at precisely the time we need it. And it will come.

Kevin was an alcoholic with two DUIs. After he ran over and killed a neighbor's dog, Kevin asked God to help him stop drinking. He expected the answer immediately and without effort, as if by magic. His prayer was answered but in the form of Alcoholics Anonymous, which required him to work hard to change himself. Yet AA brought so many benefits that he

was ultimately grateful not only for his sobriety but for AA and the work
that had made it possible.

How to Pray

We have explored five types of prayer in terms of content, but the question
remains: What is the mechanism of prayer? How does one pray? Since
prayer is a conversation with God, we open that conversation by praying
to the God of our understanding, whatever that understanding is. We may
address God by our chosen name or term, or we may use no name at all. If
we are open to prayer but don't believe in God, we can pray "to whom it
may concern." We can even begin our prayer with, "I don't believe in you,
but . . ." All of us have seen the power of love in our lives, so we can pray to
love. The term doesn't matter. Prayer works regardless of how we address
the higher power.

Although prayer is a conversation with God, no specific words are prescribed as long as they are sincere and authentic. We say what we need to
say in our own words, making the prayer as simple or elaborate as we want.
We can even begin with, "I feel very awkward doing this, but . . ." Although many beautiful prayers have been written over the centuries across
all the religions of the world, we can believe that no words are more beautiful to God than the heartfelt words we offer in moments of need and
thanksgiving. Some people get down on their knees to pray because it reminds them that prayer is a sacred moment. Others kneel as a way of expressing their humility before God. Other people stand. Many people sit.
Prayers can be said from any position with equally good effect. The traditional way to end a prayer in the Western tradition is with "amen," a He-
brew word meaning "to trust" that was used to indicate acceptance of what
someone had said or as approval for a course of action. The use of amen
signals that our prayer has ended.

When we take our problems to God in prayer, it is like taking them, as
a child, to a trusted and loving parent. We know God will solve them, but
the solution will be determined by God, not by us. Although we may
think that we know the best solution and the answer we want to our

prayer, we don't know it. We can't know it, because we cannot see to the end of our lives or beyond. Nor can we know, in an ultimate sense, what is best for others for whom we pray despite our belief that we do. For these reasons, an appropriate closing for every prayer is, "Your will, not mine, be done," leaving open the possibility of something happening that is much better than we could have imagined for ourselves or others.

The Role of Prayer in Letting Go of Regret

Prayer can be used to help you achieve specific goals related to each of the steps. For example, one of the uses of prayer is to help you do something that you couldn't otherwise do or to do it more thoroughly, with greater ease, and with less fear. In working each step, you will create specific prayers tailored to the step and to your needs related to that step. For example, in a given step, you might pray for:

- Courage to overcome your fear of working the step.
- Strength to start the step and the perseverance to complete it.
- Support and encouragement for what you are doing through the words, presence, and friendship of others.
- The insights and recall you need to carry out the activities of the step.
- Solutions for problems you encounter in working the step.

Each step and its activities will present its own challenges that prayer can help you overcome. In every case, the most effective prayer will be the one you create from the heart.

Answered Prayers

When we complain that God has not answered our prayers, what we really mean is that God has not given us the answer we wanted.

God always answers our prayers. Sometimes the answer is yes, sometimes the answer is "Not now, but when you are ready," and sometimes the answer is no. The only answer we really like is the first one, but we often get the second or the third answer. When we get the second or third, we often say that God hasn't answered our prayers, and we feel abandoned or deprived. Why we do not get what we want and why we are sometimes made to suffer are two of the great mysteries of our existence. Most faith traditions attempt to explain them in one way or another, but we cannot know for sure, because that knowledge is denied to us as human beings. One possible explanation is that the second or third answers are given to us because we need them. Just as small children do not always get what they want for their own sakes, we may not get everything we want for our own sakes. That's hard to believe when our prayer was to spare the life of a child. Yet, we don't know why our request was denied. All we know is that we did not get the answer we wanted, and we are disappointed, even deeply saddened that we didn't. That does not mean, however, that God has abandoned us, only that the answer to our prayer was no for reasons that we may never understand.

Sometimes our prayer is answered but not in the way we wanted. When prayer does not change the external conditions of our lives, it often changes us instead. When we are changed, we will see external conditions differently. We may understand them better, become reconciled to them, and experience gratitude where only bitterness had existed before. Or we find a different solution to our problem, and new roads open up that take us to a destination we had always dreamed of reaching. The answer to our prayer may not be the answer we wanted, but it may be the answer we needed, which we can often confirm after a sufficient passage of time.

Sometimes our prayer is answered, but the solution isn't obvious. While the solution to a problem may come suddenly in a single event or insight, it may also come slowly or indirectly through unanticipated channels. Other people or a gradual realization may unexpectedly lead us to new choices and new experiences that provide the help we were seeking. We will not see the subtle or complex answer to our prayer, however, unless we are open to it. Being open and receptive are therefore essential aspects of prayer. The answer to a prayer for a better job, for example, might come as a recommendation or opportunity for additional education, something we had not previously considered or even wanted to undertake.

The Evidence on Prayer

The anecdotal evidence on the effectiveness of prayer is clear. It works. In other words, there are countless stories of the power of prayer to change individuals and their lives. But is there any scientific evidence? Is there any way to prove that prayer works? Perhaps surprisingly, this subject is an area of growing interest to academic researchers, especially within the last decade. Ten years ago there were 3 U.S. medical schools out of 125 that had courses examining the role that prayer, religious devotion, and spirituality played in health. Today there are 60, with about 100 more indicating that they will offer them in the future. In 2000 the National Institutes of Health launched a five-year study to determine if meditative prayer said twice a day could improve the health of breast cancer patients—a study that would have been inconceivable ten years ago. Research on prayer and religion in health is a young field, but it is growing rapidly.

To date, the results of scientific studies indicate that people who pray regularly and attend religious services are healthier, live longer, and have significantly lower blood pressure than those who do not. Other studies have shown that prayer and faith speed recovery from depression, alcoholism, hip surgery, drug addiction, stroke, rheumatoid arthritis, heart attacks, and bypass surgery. Approximately 99 percent of family physicians believe that personal prayer, meditation, or other spiritual and religious practices can boost medical treatment. While many more studies will be needed to provide evidence of the specific effects of prayer, the early studies are fascinating and suggestive. Approximately 90 percent of Americans report that they pray.

Sharing with Others

The practice of sharing our emotional lives with someone else brings many benefits. Some of the benefits of purposeful sharing related to our regrets are these:

- Sharing allows us to test our own understanding of our regrets against the reality of another person's perspective and experience.

- Sharing limits the impact of our regret-related fears, because it forces us to identify and examine them. Such analysis puts boundaries around them, which makes them less frightening, more manageable, and easier to release.
- Sharing allows us to access additional counsel as we work the steps and choose among alternative actions.
- Sharing brings someone else in our lives to provide the emotional and psychological support we need to help us address our regrets and then to let them go.
- Sharing reduces our isolation. It opens us to feelings of being valued and loved, which are healing gifts.

In Step Two, you will choose a confidant with whom to share your journey of letting go. While there may be many people with whom you can share parts of your story and find the insight, wisdom, and emotional support you need, your confidant will be a special person who understands and supports what you are trying to do. He or she will know more about your regrets than anyone else and will be an active participant in helping you work the steps.

Affirmations

Affirmations are an effective tool for bringing about a change in your perspective and, therefore, in your circumstances. *An affirmation is a written or spoken statement made in language that is clear, positive, and concise that a desired future state is already in existence.* Perhaps the granddaddy of all affirmations was created by Émile Coué, a French psychotherapist. His affirmation was so popular that it became a national phenomenon that swept America in the 1920s. Still effective for general purposes today, Coué's affirmation is: "Every day in every way, I am getting better and better."

The mechanism of affirmations is not entirely understood. Apparently, often-repeated affirmations are received by our unconscious mind as fact rather than fantasy, which leads it to conclude that what we want to happen has already happened. It may be that such a belief facilitates our bringing about the event (for example, not smoking), or perhaps there are other forces at work.

Affirmations counter negative head talk, which generates fear, feelings of incompetence, and a sense of worthlessness. When we become stressed, afraid, or angry about our regrets and their consequences, affirmations calm us, providing internal support that is loving and reassuring. Affirmations have the advantage of being short and quick. They can be said aloud in the isolation of a room, alone in an automobile, or silently to oneself in a crowded office or grocery store.

The following guidelines will help you create effective affirmations:

- Keep the affirmation as concise and simple as possible, and make clear the desired future state that you are seeking. For example, "I accept responsibility for my own happiness" is preferable to "I am confident that I will come to see that my current state of unhappiness is not the fault of others but of myself."
- Use only positive statements that affirm something rather than negative statements that deny something. For example, "I have forgiven my ex-husband" rather than "I don't hold a grudge against my ex-husband anymore."
- Choose words and phrases that you are comfortable using and that seem natural to you. The words do not have to be fancy or elaborate.
- Make the statement in the present tense so that it sounds as if the future state you are seeking already exists. Do not use the future tense. The objective is to communicate to your unconscious mind that whatever it is you want has already come true. For example, "I accept that I did the best I could at the time" rather than "I will try to accept that I did the best I could at the time."
- Believe that what you are affirming is possible and also that it is true.

Affirmations are not commands to ourselves but observations about our lives. We are not ordering ourselves to become something but confirming that what we want already is. Affirmations can be said at any time, but they are especially effective when we are relaxed, such as when we are waking up in the morning or going to sleep at bedtime. Affirmations can be written as well as spoken. Write the affirmation in long-hand twenty or thirty times on a sheet of paper, thinking carefully about the words. Believe that what you are writing is already true, feel the pleasure that the words evoke, and enjoy the effect that the affirmation describes.

Creative Visualization

As human beings, we are constantly visualizing to ourselves. We visualize whenever we leave the present moment to jump into the future, return to the past, or think about a friend. Visualization is a constant companion and a natural part of living. It is also an essential component of regretting. Whenever we go back to our regrets or imagine their effects on our future, we are visualizing. We have left the present moment and journeyed through time. When that journey to regret leaves us with recurring sadness about the past or fear about the future, it has been a counterproductive visualization. Those of us with regrets create visualizations like those all the time. What we need are more productive visualizations. The good news is that we can create them.

The visualization that takes us back and leaves us stranded in the past or propels us to loneliness or imagined danger in the future can be harnessed to serve another purpose. It can be used to heal our past, enrich our present, and reconfigure our future. Purposeful visualization is an extraordinary tool for changing—and healing—our lives. It is a skill we can master that will help us let go of our regrets. The process of intentionally creating vividly imagined scenes to bring about specific changes in our lives and ourselves is called *creative visualization.* It is a process through which we use our imagination consciously, creatively, and specifically to imagine things differently, to imagine them the way we want them to be.

In creative visualization, we create in our mind's eye an imagined situation with as many effects of real life as we feel comfortable including—sounds, colors, tastes, physical sensations, smells. Our goal is to make the visualization as realistic and convincing as possible. Although we are constructing scenes filled with realistic details, what we are visualizing is something that has not yet come to pass. We are imagining the future in order to manifest that future in our present lives.

Creative visualizations can be thought of as visual affirmations or even focused daydreams. They are not dreams because they are conscious rather than unconscious. They are not hallucinations because they are intentional and we know that they are imaginary. They are not ordinary daydreams because they are not for entertainment but to achieve a specific future state that we want to bring about.

Theories on why visualization works are varied, covering a wide range of disciplines. Science, religion, and New Age thinkers all have explanations. So did the ancient Greeks, and so do contemporary scientists. No one knows for sure why visualizations work, only that they do. Creative visualization has proven effective in divergent applications with considerably different stakes, from treating serious illness to improving one's golf swing.

We know that visualization works in part because the construction of the mind is such that it cannot tell the difference between a vividly imagined scene and one that actually takes place. So when we create scenes of future states that we want to bring about, the mind experiences them as real. That's one reason why visualizations reduce our fear of change and move us closer to what we want to have or to be. Because we have already "lived it," we are not as afraid, and the reality does not seem as foreign or as unlikely to us.

Another purpose that visualization serves is training. Sports figures repeatedly imagine themselves playing the perfect game as a means of improving their game. In their mind, it's as if they have already played perfectly, so they know how to do it and are even practiced at doing it. For that reason, visualizations play an important part in their professional training. Using the same technique, we can prepare ourselves to make amends, to let go of regrets, and to grant forgiveness. Yet there is still a mystery about how creative visualization works, especially when it results in profound changes that seem beyond our own capabilities to bring about.

Two very good books describe how to use creative visualization for purposes of healing: Patrick Fanning's *Visualization for Change,* which is a detailed handbook on creative visualization, and Shakti Gawain's *Creative Visualization*, which takes a somewhat different approach to describing the process. Both books are listed in appendix A, "Recommended Reading." This chapter provides general guidelines for using creative visualizations, but it cannot completely substitute for the thoroughness of these books. You may want to read them as well.

Guidelines for Visualizing

Creative visualization is not difficult. The following guidelines will increase the effectiveness of every visualization exercise that you do.

1. *Determine the objective of the visualization.*

    What specifically is it that you are attempting to accomplish with this visualization? Is it to let go of a specific resentment, to forgive another person for a certain act, to encourage yourself to work a step, or to forgive yourself for holding onto a regret? Whatever the objective, it must be clear because it will define the content of your visualization.

2. *Determine the content of the visualization.*

    What picture can you create in your mind that will capture what you are trying to bring about? One approach is to imagine the scene with the literal events taking place before your eyes. You could imagine yourself, for example, apologizing to an individual you had harmed, saying the very words you would say in the very room in which you expect to say them. An alternative approach is to create a metaphor or analogy for what you are trying to achieve with the visualization.

    A metaphor is something that acts as a symbol to represent something else. For example, you could choose a small bird held in your hand as a metaphor for your regrets. In the visualization, you could see yourself opening your hand to release the bird—and your regrets. Then, with pleasure, you would watch the bird fly away, never to return, leaving you happy and without regret. A metaphor is preferable to a literal representation when the metaphor feels more comfortable or when a literal visualization would be too complex to capture what you are trying to achieve.

3. *Eliminate distractions.*

Find a quiet place, close the door, unplug the phone, tell others in your house to leave you alone, use earplugs, or do whatever else you need to do so that you will not be distracted during the visualization.

4. *Get comfortable.*

Assume a comfortable position for your visualization. Recline on the sofa, lie on your back, sit in a chair, or choose some other position that is comfortable and relaxing for you.

5. *Close your eyes.*

Close your eyes to focus your attention inward and to shut out the visual distractions of the world. Since you will be creating your own visualizations on the blank screen of your mind, competing visual images from the real world should be eliminated.

6. *Relax.*

With your eyes closed, enter into a state of relaxation. Release the anxieties, worries, fears, and obsessions of the day. Feel them drain out of you. If necessary, use one of the many exercises that can induce relaxation. A simple such exercise is to breathe deeply, counting slowly backward from ten. With each number, feel yourself sinking deeper and deeper into a relaxed state. A more elaborate approach is to tighten and relax each major muscle of your body, one at a time, beginning with those in the hands and concluding with those in the feet, feeling your relaxation deepen with each muscle tightened and released. Since your most natural periods of relaxation are just before falling asleep and just after waking, these two times of the day are highly effective for creative visualizations.

7. *Create the visual image.*

The purpose of creative visualization is to bring into existence a future state that you desire. The more vivid the imagery of that future state, the more effective the visualization is likely to be, because the more real it will seem to your mind. Follow these guidelines for creating powerful visual images.

- Imagine the future state you want to come about, experiencing it as if it were already true.
- Feel the emotions appropriate to the visualization, because they will make it more real to the mind.
- Include as many senses as possible in the visualization: sight, sound, smell, taste, and touch.
- Include as many details as possible, including imagined conversations and actions.
- If negative thoughts or images arise, imagine them floating down a river and drifting out of sight with no energy given them. Or imagine a big "Cancelled" stamp descending on them. Use whatever image appeals to you as a way of voiding, neutralizing, or ignoring intruding thoughts or images.
- Maintain this state of imagining for as long as you wish.

8. *End with an affirmation.*

End each visualization with an affirmation that allows something better than you had imagined to come into being. For example, you might close with, "This or something better is now happening for me for the benefit of all concerned in accordance with God's will."

The more you desire what you are visualizing, the more you believe in its realization, and the more willing you are to accept that realization, the more likely the visualization is to manifest. Ironically, you can increase your willingness to believe in the realization and to accept it through visualizing.

Summary of Visualization Guidelines

1. Determine the objective of the visualization.
2. Determine the content of the visualization.
3. Eliminate distractions.
4. Get comfortable.

5. Close your eyes.
6. Relax.
7. Create the visual image.
8. End with an affirmation.

Creative Visualization and the Steps

Creative visualization can be applied in many different ways in working the steps, but three ways are especially important. Each of the three ways makes it easier for you to work the step because, in a sense, you have already "worked" it in your mind. Three uses for creative visualization in step work are in:

1. Preparing for the step.
2. Carrying out different activities specified in the step.
3. Facilitating the use of other spiritual and psychological tools while working the step.

PREPARING FOR THE STEP

The use of creative visualization at the beginning of a step can help you work that step with lower resistance, less fear, and greater confidence. Use creative visualization immediately after completing the previous step to prepare for the next one and again after reading about the new step itself. The design of a creative visualization used at the start of a step might include the following elements. Visualize yourself:

- Reading the step and feeling enthusiastic about doing it.
- Going over each of the activities in the step, knowing that you can do them all.
- Completing each of the activities.
- Congratulating yourself on completing the step.
- Hearing your confidant tell you how well you have worked the step.
- Feeling happy and rewarded for finishing the step.
- Looking forward to the next step.

CARRYING OUT STEP ACTIVITIES

Creative visualization can be a powerful tool in helping you overcome resistance to carrying out step activities. It can be used to overcome fear, stimulate your memory, and develop creative solutions to the problems you encounter in working the step. When you face an activity that is frightening, for example, visualize yourself starting the activity, losing your fear, growing increasingly excited as you make progress on it, and completing the activity with a sense of satisfaction and accomplishment. See yourself encouraged by your confidant and others along the way and congratulated by yourself at the successful conclusion of the activity. The content of each visualization will differ slightly, of course, depending upon the nature of that activity.

FACILITATING THE USE OF OTHER SPIRITUAL AND PSYCHOLOGICAL TOOLS

Creative visualization can be used to encourage your use of other spiritual and psychological tools or to encourage their more frequent use in working the steps. For example, if you are resistant to praying, visualize yourself praying. Visualize the act of prayer and the results of prayer: feeling supported, less anxious, more confident, and happier. If you are resistant to journaling, visualize yourself writing in a journal. Feel yourself receiving the emotional rewards that come from journaling, such as a reduction in fear, an increase in hope, and greater clarity about your situation.

If you are resistant to sharing your life with others, visualize yourself sharing it and feeling the sense of community, the warmth of another's love, and the courage to continue in your efforts that come with revealing part of yourself to someone who cares about you. See yourself embraced by the other person, listened to sympathetically, and supported emotionally. Feel the surge in confidence and hope. If you are resistant to making affirmations, visualize yourself making affirmations regularly, enjoying them, and profiting from them in ways that you specify in the visualization.

In the same way that you can use visualizations to increase your use of prayer, you can use prayer to increase your use of creative visualization. A simple prayer for this purpose might be: "Please help me to use creative visualization in working this step and to use it frequently so that I can complete the step successfully, according to your will." You can also use affirmations to encourage your use of creative visualization as in, "I am using creative visualizations in this step."

Your mastery of the spiritual and psychological tools will improve with practice. Eventually their use will become second nature to you and their rewards a continuing gift. The more tools you use and the more often you use them, the greater the likelihood that you will let go of your regrets and that you will do so in less time and with greater ease than would otherwise be the case.

With this chapter, your period of preparation has come to an end. You are now ready to work Step One, which begins your journey through the steps to the freedom from regret that you seek.

PART II

THE TEN STEPS TO LETTING GO OF REGRET

4

STEP ONE: LISTING REGRETS

THE STRUCTURED PROGRAM of the Ten Steps will lead you through the process of letting go of your regrets. Supported by the spiritual and psychological tools, you will come to terms with those regrets, release the painful emotions they are causing, and end the distortions they are creating in your life. One page at a time, one day at a time, one step at a time, you will journey along a healing path to freedom from the burden of your regrets.

The more complete and dedicated your step work, the more effective it will be. Realistically, however, even a modest effort on every step will produce beneficial results in reducing the power of your regrets to hurt you. Therefore, it is better to work the Ten Steps, putting forth some effort than to abandon them and make no effort at all. On the other hand, because you have the opportunity to let go of the burdensome regrets of your life, it would be preferable to be thorough and dedicated from the very start.

As you will recall from chapter 2, to work a step means:

- To understand the purpose of the step and its role in letting go of your regrets.
- To take the actions the step recommends, applying its principles to your life and changing your behavior accordingly.

The purpose of Step One is to identify and describe the burdensome regrets that you want to let go. These are the regrets that you return to repetitively—regrets that are intense and painful, that steal the joy from the present, and condemn you again to the sufferings of the past. These are the regrets that have led you to this book. Listing them is the first step in letting them go.

Working Step One

Each step has an "Action List" to guide you through the journaling exercises and other activities associated with the step. All Ten Steps should be worked for each burdensome regret. However, you have a choice as to how you do that. You may choose to take only one regret at a time and apply all the steps to that regret. In other words, only after you have let go of one regret do you begin on the next. Conversely, you may prefer to work each step on several or all of your regrets simultaneously. The choice is yours; both approaches are effective.

In completing the Action List items for Step One, you may choose to identify all your regrets at once (so that you will have a complete list), or you may name only the first regret on which you intend to work the steps. The choice is yours, but the option of listing all your regrets is generally preferable.

The Action List for Step One is shown in the following box.

Action List: Step One

Listing Regrets

1. Name of the regret
2. Description of the regret
3. Category of the regret
4. Feelings about the regret
5. "If onlys"

The purpose of the five journaling activities on the Action List is to take you through an analytical process that will result in a complete description of each of your regrets. Address these items in whatever order you want, but apply all five to each of your regrets. Don't be concerned about fine distinctions among them.

The following paragraphs describe each activity in more detail so that you will know how to complete it.

1. Name of the Regret

Choose a shorthand name that you will use to refer to the regret throughout the steps. You may change this name whenever you want.

2. Description of the Regret

Describe each regret, its major events, its causes, and its consequences. What happened (or didn't happen) that you now regret? What were the results? Steve, for example, regretted the death of his parents in a car accident when he was seven. That regret led to others, including being handed off from relative to relative and foster parent to foster parent until he was eighteen. Steve regretted the accompanying financial insecurity, the unpredictable home life, and the many different schools he was forced to attend. He regretted being "different," not knowing for sure where he would live the following year and having no one to confide in whom he really trusted. Steve longed for a set of loving parents, a stable home, and friends that he had known for more than a year.

Should the process of describing your regrets grow painful, return to the spiritual and psychological tools for support. For example, you can journal about how much it hurts to analyze your regrets in such detail; how you wish you didn't have to do it; the fears that arise when you remember all that happened; how angry you feel; how difficult this is; how unfair you think life is; or anything else you feel about your regrets or the process. You can also journal about the hopes you have for what you are doing, the benefits of letting go of your regrets, and the confidence you have that you will get through the steps to find a new freedom and happiness.

You may wish to pray to your higher power, asking for the courage and strength to complete this step. Ask for divine support to handle the fear and the pain you feel. If you need to cry, by all means cry. Courage in dealing with regrets means being willing to express your feelings, not stifle them.

Use creative visualization to move through the step and facilitate your progress. Breathe deeply. Imagine yourself sitting in front of your journal, remembering the past, but protected from fear and harm. See yourself recalling your regrets, describing their causes and consequences, knowing that it is safe for you to do so. Imagine yourself writing with confidence, completing the step, feeling good about it, and then moving on to the next step.

3. Category of the Regret

Categorize each regret according to the categories described in chapter 1 and below. The purpose of this exercise is to increase your understanding of the regret by labeling it. The seven categories are:

1. Acts you committed (but wish you hadn't)
2. Acts you didn't commit (but wish you had)
3. Acts others committed (that you wish they hadn't)
4. Acts others didn't commit (that you wish they had)
5. Acts of fate or circumstances
6. Inevitable losses (that you regret)
7. Comparisons (that lead you to regret)

In some cases, a regret may fall into more than one category. When it does, list each category that applies.

4. Feelings about the Regret

Emotions power our lives and make them meaningful. Without emotions, we would be incapable of intimacy and, surprisingly, even of reasoning.

We could conceptualize options but not choose among them. We could recount the events of our lives but not the feelings that accompanied them. We would be incapable of maintaining relationships, motivating ourselves, or planning our future. We would be less than human. Emotion creates hope and expectation, produces understanding and purpose, and generates empathy and wisdom. It is emotion that speaks to our souls when we confront eternity, that thrills us in the act of loving, and that leads us to transcendent experiences. It is emotion that complements rational thought to provide the totality of the human experience, that gives the truest expression to what it means to be alive.

But while our emotions enrich our lives, they also complicate them. They lead us into bad decisions, seduce us into states of unhappiness or despair, and render the past a thing of the present. Tyrannical and unforgiving, like cruel wardens or harsh taskmasters, emotions can coerce or cripple us, depriving us of the things we long for most. While some of us have learned to manage our emotions well, others are managed by their emotions, victims rather than beneficiaries.

Emotions play a big role in harboring regrets and in letting them go. To release the regrets that imprison us, we must come to terms with them intellectually, but we must also come to terms with them emotionally. We cannot just think our regrets away. We also have to feel them away, allowing the emotions that surround them to touch us but not to disable us. If our emotions are to serve us rather than dominate us, we must develop some understanding of how to manage them effectively.

Part of working the Ten Steps, therefore, entails learning to be aware of your emotions and to marshal them in the service of letting go of your regrets. It is unfelt emotions, not felt emotions, that you cannot change and, therefore, that exercise a hidden power over you. When you recognize an emotion, you can connect it to the thought or event that created it. Once you connect the emotion to its source, you can use your thinking mind to limit it, increase it, or change it. This is thought analysis. For example, if you feel fear at the thought of journaling about your regrets, you can use your rational mind to limit the fear by reassuring yourself. You can tell yourself that journaling is the right action to take, that it will turn out well, and that you have the strength and courage to overcome the fear you feel. You can remind yourself that the journaling activities in each step are essential to working the step and to letting go of your regrets. You can remind yourself of the future benefits that you will receive from journaling and completing the steps—thereby increasing your motivation—and comfort yourself in your fear, thereby making it more manageable. Whenever you identify an emotion that might impede your progress, counteract it through rational thought, using the tool of thought analysis.

The better we are at recognizing and managing our own emotions, the better we will be at recognizing the emotions we see in others. This capacity to identify with and understand the emotions of others is empathy. Empathy allows us to have meaningful and productive relationships. It also facilitates forgiveness, because it enables us to identify with the feelings, limitations, and imperfections of those who have hurt us and so to develop sympathy for them. How we relate to others and how we relate to ourselves are inextricably interwoven. The more compassion, acceptance, and empathy we have for others, the more compassion and acceptance we will have for ourselves. Empathy is one of the emotional capacities that will serve us well in letting go of our regrets.

The Feelings of Regret

Regret is not a simple feeling but a complex one. It is really a constellation of feelings, which is one reason regrets are so difficult to bear. In examining the feelings we have about our regrets, we will concentrate on six:

1. Anger
2. Fear
3. Guilt
4. Shame
5. Pain (including hurt, sadness, remorse, and grief)
6. Longing

There are other feelings that may surface, such as disgust or even joy at the unexpected kindnesses we experienced as our regret unfolded. But most of the other feelings that emerge, like rage or vengeance, are some variation of these six.

Anger and *fear* need no introduction. Most of us know these feelings well. Some of the other feelings may not be as clear to us. *Guilt,* for example, is the emotion we feel when we have done something that violates our value system. Our capacity for guilt motivates us to behave appropriately and to make amends when we do not. Guilt is a good thing when it is deserved and in proper proportion. We encounter problems with guilt when it is excessive or assumed but not deserved. Cho takes on guilt even when she has no real reason to feel guilty. Her family members and coworkers know of this susceptibility and use it regularly to manipulate her. Cho has many regrets stemming from her exaggerated sense of guilt.

Shame is often part of guilt, but it is useful to think of it as a different emotion. We feel guilt when we have *done* something wrong, such as lie or steal. Shame, on the other hand, comes not from the unworthiness of the action but from the unworthiness of ourselves. While guilt is about action, shame is about us and who we are as human beings. Shame is more troubling than guilt because it tells us that we are bad people, not good people doing bad things.

Deep shame is a component of many regrets. With such shame, we cannot separate what we have done from who we are, and we think of ourselves as fundamentally flawed, profoundly inferior, terribly unworthy. We mix shame with guilt in a toxic combination, even taking on guilt that is not rightly ours. "I could never be forgiven," we say of our regrets. Or, "I don't deserve to be happy." Our regrets have come to define us, not in terms of what we *did* but in terms of who we *are*.

Each of us is a precious creature of our higher power. Each of us was created of equal value, and we retain that value in the eyes of God or whatever term we use for transcendent forces. Not one of us is worthless. We may earn the praise and admiration of our fellows or we may not, but material achievements do not affect our worth in the only realm that counts: the realm of the spirit. My favorite expression in this regard is, "God doesn't make junk." And, indeed, God doesn't.

Pain is another critical emotion in letting go of regrets because it is part of every regret and because, ironically, it is one path to healing. Pain comes in many forms: physical, spiritual, and emotional. Emotional pain can be experienced as grief, sadness, loneliness, longing, or unhappiness. We feel it as agony or angst, as misery or anguish, as suffering or torment. Pain is something that most of us try hard to avoid. Yet pain brings us a priceless gift when we are willing to experience it. Ironically, it is the same gift that joy brings. It is the gift of healing.

Most of us have experienced the therapeutic benefits of a good cry. When we express our pain, we experience the physical and emotional relief that comes from that expression, and we begin to heal. When we refuse to express the pain, we remain trapped in that pain and cannot be healed. Until we consciously and willingly experience our pain, we cannot get past it. The only way to the other side of pain is through it. It cannot be circumvented or its effects avoided by refusing to feel it. Pain has to be confronted, felt, and walked through to be released.

Longing is often prevalent in our regrets. Longing is a persistent yearning for something, usually for something that cannot be attained. Many of us who regret deeply have a terrible longing for what might have been. It is captured in our recurring thoughts that begin, "If only . . ." The devastating loss we feel from broken promises, failed expectations, and lost hopes is an intense expression of pain and sadness. In an attempt to escape the excruciating pain, we long for what could have been, retreating to fantasies that begin, "If only. . . ."

Our emotions define our experience as human beings and, within a broad range, are controllable by us. They are partners with our rational mind in determining how we experience life and how well we handle our regrets. Every feeling, at one time or another, is a legitimate response to life, but only those emotions that are felt can be managed by our thinking mind and resolved. If we deny or suppress our feelings without experiencing them or if we allow them to overwhelm us, we will be their victims rather than their beneficiaries.

In this Action List item, acknowledge the feelings you have about your regret: the fear, pain, anger, sorrow, guilt, and shame you associate with it. Be thorough and honest. By capturing these emotions in writing, you are reducing their power to hurt you, taming them so that you can learn from them and let them go. If the journaling process becomes too painful, use visualization, prayer, thought analysis, affirmations, and the love of others to support you in continuing.

5. "If Onlys"

This journal entry is not the history of a regret but the fantasy of it. Instead of a description of your regret, it is a description of its opposite: of what might have been, of what "should" have been or "could" have been, "if only . . ." "If onlys" describe what you wish had happened rather than what did happen with your regret. These are the fantasies you have when you indulge thoughts that begin, "If only I had" or "If only I hadn't," "If only they had" or "If only they hadn't."

When her fiancé broke off their engagement, Isabel regretted the collapse of their relationship, the embarrassment, and the time she had invested in loving him. Later, however, she regretted the things that might have been: the children, the home, and the joys they could have shared. Isabel's fantasized outcomes were predictions about how good things would be today *if only they had been different then*. She blamed this regret for her present unhappiness and for the big things she had been denied in life but would have had "if only . . ."

Describe the fantasy outcomes that you hold for your regrets. What are your "if onlys"? What do you believe would have been different if the regret that now burdens you had never occurred?

With the completion of Step One, you now possess a comprehensive description of all your burdensome regrets. As bad as they may seem, what you see before you summarizes all there is with which you have to deal. This is the complete picture of your regrets. And it is manageable.

Step Two continues the analytical process with a more detailed examination of each regret so that you can begin to let it go. But first, take a break and do something fun. You deserve it.

5

STEP TWO: EXAMINING REGRETS

"THE LIFE THAT IS UNEXAMINED," Plato wrote, "is not worth living." And a regret that is unexamined is not worth keeping. One of the reasons that people hold onto their regrets is that they have not examined them closely. Until they look at their regrets with a logical eye, they are powerless over them. Once they have identified and examined them, however, they are in a position to understand them better, and they can use that understanding to let them go. Therefore, Step Two is about analyzing each of your regrets, your role in creating it, and the circumstances that surrounded its creation. In this step you will also identify a trustworthy person (your confidant) with whom to share your journey of letting go.

Preparation for the Step

The process of letting go of your regrets is more likely to be effective when it is undertaken in the company of others. The more people you trust to help you, the more support you will find for the tasks you will undertake. Whether you involve one person or a small group in your journey, the emotional sustenance and the psychological insights they provide will motivate and reassure you. Human beings are meant to live in community. This experience of sympathetic support will strengthen your resolve, support your effort to change, and give you the love you need to keep moving forward.

If you have little experience in sharing your life with others, you will need courage to reach out. But you can pray for that courage, visualize it, affirm it, and journal about it. When you apply the spiritual and psychological tools, amazing things will happen to give you the opportunities you need and the courage you seek. You will find yourself doing things you didn't think you could do—and not quite knowing how you could do them. Spiritual forces will rally to help you, and people will appear to assist you. Encouragement, support, and insights will come from unexpected places—an old friend, a new acquaintance, an article in a magazine you chanced to read. You are never alone when you are trying to grow spiritually—never alone because powerful forces ally to help you. That does not mean that your journey will be fearless, painless, or easy. It does mean that you will be given all the courage you need to overcome your fear and all the strength you need to overcome the pain and difficulties you encounter on the journey.

Finding a Confidant

Regardless of whether or not you choose to share your journey with friends or members of a small group, you need to identify one person in whom to confide and with whom you will work the steps. This person will be your designated confidant. Your confidant is someone you trust to share the intimate aspects of your journey and who will assist you in working the Ten Steps. Your confidant will challenge or support your decisions, as appropriate, and help you clarify your options as you progress through the steps. Because your confidant will play such a vital role, you must choose him or her with care.

Your designated confidant should be someone:

- Who is a good listener.
- With whom you are comfortable in confiding.
- Whose judgment you trust.
- Who has your best interests at heart.

- Who will maintain the confidentiality of what you say.
- Who will never use anything you tell him or her against you.
- Who will honor your emotions and let you have them without being embarrassed or distressed.

In thinking about someone to fulfill that role, whom might you consider? List the names of possible candidates in your journal.

Also give some thought to others with whom you might share portions of your journey of letting go, not as your designated confidant, but as fellow travelers or potential members of a small group of people devoted to letting go of their regrets. Use your journal to list the names of these people.

Using the Spiritual and Psychological Tools

Step Two can be a painful and discouraging step unless you make use of the spiritual and psychological tools. Use the tools in preparation for the step as well as for each item on the Action List. Pray for the courage to face your regrets honestly and squarely, to remember accurately the past actions and events that contributed to them, and to see all the consequences you've suffered from holding onto them. Ask your higher power to keep you from false blame or from denying your own role in the events that triggered your regret. Pray that you will find the emotional support you need as you return to your regrets and reconstruct them for the purpose of letting them go. Pray to be comforted, to be loved, and to know that things will work for the best, confident that you will find your way to a happy ending at the conclusion of this process.

Visualize yourself starting the step, working it with courage and determination, and feeling a sense of release and accomplishment at its successful completion. Imagine yourself beginning and finishing each of the items on the Action List, being praised by your confidant for a job well done, and congratulating yourself on what you have accomplished. Imagine the confidence you feel having catalogued and so contained your regrets—with all their consequences and blame and anger clearly listed.

Imagine the joy that comes from facing your past squarely and knowing that the remaining steps, like this step, will lead you to freedom.

Journal about your fears and your anger whenever they arise. Write about the sadness you feel, how much remembering still hurts, and how much you want to let go of the pain. Remind yourself in your journal, using thought analysis, of the many benefits that will come as a result of your courageous actions in completing this step. Journal about your hopes for the future and about your commitment to completing this step.

Share your pain and your fear with your confidant, revealing whatever you need to communicate in order to be helped, supported, and encouraged. Ask for sympathy and emotional support from your friends as you work the step, and use your confidant as a sounding board to explore the many negative consequences of holding onto your regrets.

Use affirmations to support you at every stage of the step. Affirm, for example, "I am successfully completing Step Two," "I am examining my regrets," "I am eagerly doing whatever is necessary to let go of my regrets," and "I am safe, loved, and supported."

Working Step Two

In Step One, you described your regrets and the feelings associated with them. In Step Two, you will analyze those regrets in more detail. As in the previous step, an Action List of items will lead you through the journaling exercises.

Action List: Step Two

Examining Regrets

1. Your role in creating the regret
2. Those you hurt in the regret
3. Those you blame for the regret
4. Consequences of holding onto the regret

I. Your Role in Creating the Regret

What part did you play in creating your regret? In some cases, your role may have been primary. Louis, for example, was extremely possessive of his fiancée. The closer they had grown emotionally, the more jealous he became of her male friends and the more suspicious he was of her activities when he was not around. Ultimately, Louis even became resentful of the time she spent with her girlfriends, preferring that she spend the time with him because he "loved her so much." When his fiancée finally broke off the engagement, because, she said, he was "suffocating" her, Louis was devastated. It was the biggest regret of his life. Only in retrospect could he admit that the responsibility for the breakup was largely his. He could not control his jealous behavior.

In many regrets, our responsibility is not nearly so obvious or complete. We did play a part in their creation that we need to recognize and for which we need to accept responsibility, but we were not the only cause of the regret. When our role was largely reactive or less significant than other parties', our task may be more difficult. Cindy stayed with her abusive husband because she had no other means of support and was afraid to leave for fear of what he would do to her and their children. When she did leave, she had terrible regrets over not having left sooner, and she blamed herself for all the pain he had caused their family. Cindy could have rationalized her part in the regret and denied any responsibility, but she chose the opposite tack and took on all of it. The truth lay somewhere in between. Cindy's task in this step was to own up to her real responsibility in the regret but not take on any that didn't properly belong to her.

In the case of some regrets, you may have played no role at all. For example, if you were hit by a drunk driver who swerved suddenly into your lane, you had no role in the regret the accident created. It is not reasonable to say that you could have avoided the accident "if only" you had stayed longer at your last appointment, done the dishes after all, or hung up a minute earlier from a telephone conversation you were having before you got into the car. You were driving safely and could not have known what was coming. You played no role in the regret.

Generally, however, we do have a role in creating or at least maintaining our regrets. Even in those cases where the other parties' roles were much greater than ours, we need to own up to whatever we have done that helped create the regret or that worsened it. When we believe that it is what others have done to us that created our regret and we have played little or no role, we need to examine the regret carefully. It is natural to blame others rather than ourselves. This effort to recognize our part in our regrets is not a search for more self-blame for the sake of blame. It is a quest for the truth and, so, for freedom. Whatever we have done, we can let it go but only if we admit it first.

Be thorough and complete in this analysis, using whatever spiritual and psychological tools you need to finish the task. Detailed accounts are painful, but they are healing for the same reason.

2. Those You Hurt in the Regret

List the major parties to each regret whom you hurt in some way. The people involved may have been totally innocent, such as children in a divorce. They may have been people whom you deliberately hurt in retaliation for their actions against you or people you hurt indirectly or accidentally as the regret unfolded. Ask yourself how you made the situation worse, failed to make it better, or otherwise behaved in ways that hurt the other party. Ignore what that person did to you.

Perhaps, in fact, you've hurt no one with your regret. Perhaps that regret arose from events or circumstances beyond your control: an abusive parent, the financial condition of your family, or a physical handicap with which you were born. In these cases, there are no mistakes to admit, no blame to confess, no responsibility to accept in creating the regret. Your regret rose entirely from something over which you had no control.

3. Those You Blame for the Regret

This exercise is designed to identify the people, events, or circumstances that you still blame in some way for your regrets. Developing this list is important because letting go of your regrets will entail coming to terms with these people, events, and circumstances. Not every party involved in a regret will be someone you still blame—or ever blamed. Children, for example, are parties to the regret of their parents' divorce, but they probably played no role in causing it. The divorce was their parents' decision, who bear full responsibility for it.

Some parties to your regret may have played a role in creating it but have long since been forgiven. They need not concern you here.

Some of the people you blame for your regrets may, in fact, be scapegoats with no real responsibility. If it feels like they bear some responsibility for what happened, however, include their names anyway. You will examine their roles later.

In addition to people, the list of those you blame may include chance, fate, bad luck, or God. Whomever or whatever you blame for any part in your regret should be listed in this Action List item, including yourself, if it applies.

The people on this list are the ones toward whom you hold a resentment. A resentment is a persistent feeling of anger, ill will, dislike, or hatred toward someone or something you blame for hurting you as the result of a real or imagined offense. Gail regretted the affair that led to the breakup of her marriage, a bitter divorce, and a much reduced lifestyle. Her resentments included her husband, who didn't give her a second chance; the man with whom she had the affair, who seduced her and then left her for another woman; her in-laws, who refused to speak to her after the adultery; her parents, who failed to support her by saying that what her husband wanted to do was up to him; fate, for having led her to the seducer; and an old friend, who she said betrayed her in an hour of need. She also listed the opposing attorney, whom she considered incredibly vicious; the judge, who didn't provide enough alimony; and her ex-husband's new wife, who had nothing to do with the breakup but whom she hated anyway.

In completing this journaling exercise, include a description of the resentment itself as well as the reasons you hold it. In other words, why do you blame the other party and for what? Be honest and complete, but do not dwell on these resentments beyond the journaling exercise, and do not fuel your anger with further thoughts of them. Identify the resentments and then leave them behind as you move to the next journaling topic. You will deal with these resentments later.

4. Consequences of Holding onto the Regret

The consequences of holding onto the regret are the consequences you are suffering today because you have not let it go. It is probably the primary reason you are reading this book and working this step.

Lola was in her sixties and so was her older sister, with whom she had intentionally not spoken in fifteen years. The death of Lola's only cousin, whom she had adored as a child, reminded her of how much she had shared with her sister in their youth and how much she regretted not seeing her. The fear of losing her sister without ever speaking to her again became a terrible burden. Lola thought back to the laughter and the escapades, to the times she had depended on her sister for support when there was no one else to whom she could turn. The parting words she had uttered at their breakup were not the last words she wanted to have said to the sister who had once been her best friend and a crucial part of her life. The more Lola thought of her sister, the sadder she grew about the current state of their relationship. Suddenly the consequences of holding onto the resentments the old regret had spawned were too great to bear.

The costs of holding onto a regret include the time you spend thinking about it, the emotional energy you invest in it, the sadness it causes, the anger it fosters, the happiness it steals from you, the new losses it creates, and, with some regrets, the guilt and shame it generates. Whatever the consequences, write them down. These consequences of holding onto your regrets will provide you with important reasons for letting them go.

With the completion of Step Two, you have examined your regrets in detail. You are now ready for Step Three, in which you will explore a set of thought patterns that create, deepen, and maintain regrets when the thought patterns are carried to an extreme. By identifying these thought patterns, you can counteract them, eliminating their role in maintaining your old regrets and in creating new ones.

6

STEP THREE: CHANGING TOXIC THOUGHT PATTERNS

IN STEP THREE, you will explore a set of common thought patterns that, when carried to an extreme, may have played a part in creating your regrets and in making them more difficult to let go. These common thought patterns, such as perfectionism, cause many small regrets in daily life. When they become a person's primary way of dealing with the world, however, they contribute to creating and maintaining burdensome regrets. In this step, you will determine what role, if any, these thought patterns play in the regrets you hold. By being aware of their contribution to your regrets, you can counteract them using thought analysis and the other spiritual and psychological tools available to you.

Working Step Three

The most common thought patterns that support major regrets when they become the primary way of interacting with the world are the following:

- Perfectionism
- Exaggerated control
- Foreseeing the future

- Knowing what others are thinking
- Personalizing events
- Incomplete comparisons
- Undeserved guilt
- Reimagining the past
- Extreme thinking
- Using regrets as justification for inaction

We develop some of these toxic thought patterns as children or teenagers. The adolescent belief in invincibility, for example, is universal. But if we never let it go, it will work against us, threatening our lives. Other toxic thought patterns came out of the dysfunctional families in which we were raised, providing our only defense against the difficult circumstances with which we had to cope. But after the dire circumstances of our young lives changed, we never let go of the thought patterns and their false beliefs. Now they no longer protect us. They punish us, but we continue to hold onto them.

The Action List for Step Three is as follows:

Action List: Step Three

Changing Toxic Thought Patterns

1. Analyze each regret for toxic thought patterns that support it
2. Use thought analysis to counter toxic thoughts that support the regret

---

I. Analyze Each Regret for Toxic Thought Patterns That Support It

As you read through the thought patterns described in the following paragraphs, ask yourself which ones, if any, apply to your regrets. Did any of these ways of thinking, carried to an extreme, create your regrets? Do any of these thought patterns keep you holding onto your regrets?

Perfectionism

Perfectionism is a common example of a thought pattern that characterizes many people to some degree, especially those who hold high expectations of themselves and others. When this thought pattern becomes the predominant factor in determining our behavior, however, it creates serious problems. While acknowledging intellectually and to others that perfection is impossible, perfectionists nonetheless behave as if it were possible. Nothing less than perfection is acceptable to them. To be less than perfect is to fail. But perfection isn't possible for any of us.

When we insist on being perfect or nearly perfect, we will be tortured by regrets over our mistakes and misjudgments. We repeatedly revisit the circumstances of our regrets to "make them right" in our heads or to berate ourselves for the errors that exposed our imperfection. "If only . . ." we plead with ourselves and reimagine the regret with the outcome we wanted. Or we mutter, "Why, why?" condemning ourselves for our stupidity, our carelessness, or our forgetfulness. We can't bear to accept our mistake and let it go. Such a course of action would require an admission of imperfection that is too painful to accept. Some of us are more demanding of perfection than others, and the most demanding of us are also the most impaired and the most pained.

Perfectionism keeps us from reaching our full potential and even from recognizing and acknowledging our legitimate talents and abilities. Ironically, many perfectionists do not achieve what they had hoped in life because they do not try. They do not try because they dare not fail. In our perfectionist minds, it is better to fail from not trying than to try and fail because we could not perform. Perfectionism thus robs us of the lessons of failure but not of failure itself. And it always creates regrets.

Erich, a college junior, doesn't start his papers until the night before they are due. He explains away his C by saying that he would have gotten an A "if only" he had had more time. The C doesn't represent a failure for Erich—a judgment on his real ability—because he never had the time to use that ability. He could have made an A, you see, except that he just didn't have the time. And if he lucked out with an A? Well, that's a testament to his extraordinary capability, so much greater than his friends who had devoted many hours to their papers. The problem for Erich is that he will not often luck out. So he will not often succeed. He might have made an A if he had spent a reasonable amount of time on the difficult paper, but he will never know. He couldn't take the chance of not getting the A; he couldn't take the chance of "failing."

Perfectionism makes our regrets more regrettable, self-forgiveness more unlikely, and what we did more abominable. Since we judge our actions by impossibly high standards, our mistakes seem far graver to us than they would to a nonperfectionist. This assessment makes it harder for us to forgive ourselves. It also makes it harder for us to appreciate that we may have done the best we could under the circumstances. Perfectionism interferes with the natural process of erring, learning, letting go, and moving on.

Are any of your regrets supported by perfectionism?

Exaggerated Control

A common thought pattern is an exaggerated sense of control over other people and the events of our lives. We have some influence over people and events, but we have little power to control them, and usually our influence on the final outcome is much less than we think. When this thought pattern is carried to an extreme, we take responsibility for all kinds of results over which we had no real control and for which we should not be held accountable. Yet we hold ourselves responsible anyway and so develop regrets. Consider this example of a harmless fantasy of the power to control events. Following the loss of his favorite football team in the Super Bowl, Ivan says, "I know why they lost. I didn't wear my red shirt. They always win when I wear my red shirt, but I left it at the cleaners and couldn't get it on the day of the Super Bowl and, well, you see the result!"

Of course, it's a joke, and, in this instance, Ivan doesn't really believe his claim to superpowers. It was a harmless fantasy expressed for fun. But Ivan deeply regrets that he didn't "save" his marriage. It ended because the mental illness of his former wife drove her to leave him. The marriage could not have been salvaged. Yet he accepts responsibility for its failure because he "should have been able to make it work." Like Ivan, we are victimized by unrealistic thoughts of exaggerated control when we blame ourselves for things that happened over which we had no real control. The result is an imagined sense of responsibility for the problem, grossly inflated guilt, and powerful regrets.

Are any of your regrets supported by an exaggerated sense of control over other people or events?

Foreseeing the Future

Astrology columns, fortune-tellers, psychics, economists, tarot card readers, and Wall Street analysts all point to our fascination with knowing the future. And why not? If we could foresee events, we could eliminate costly mistakes, avoid serious pain, and guarantee extraordinary success. But we cannot predict the future. Undoubtedly, there are a few people who, for whatever reason, can sometimes foresee what is going to happen. But even they are not infallible, and even they are caught unprepared by events in their own lives.

Yet in our regrets, we often blame ourselves for not having predicted future events and acted to prevent them or take advantage of them in some way. In such regretting, we blame ourselves for our "mistakes" that resulted purely from our inability to predict the future. Any regret that is based on a failure to predict the future is an unfounded regret. Alfredo, for example, blamed himself for not selling his stock in time to avoid heavy losses when the stock market declined. "I should have known that the market was going down and cashed out," he kept telling himself as he switched his now reduced stock portfolio into a cash account. Later, when the market rallied and he had not invested in it, Alfredo blamed himself for not having foreseen its rise. "I should have seen the turnaround coming," he complained bitterly to himself. But why? Why should Alfredo have known the future direction of the stock market?

The best economists and market analysts on Wall Street can't consistently predict the upward or downward movement of the stock market. The stock market goes up when people are buying more stocks than they are selling, and it goes down when people are selling more stocks than they are buying. That's the only explanation for the rise or fall of the market. Morning-after explanations of the market's direction attempt to explain *why* more people bought or sold, but these factors were not predictors the day before *because they weren't known.* The majority of professional money managers can't regularly predict the movement of the market (which is why most mutual funds don't beat the Dow Jones Industrial Average). Neither can we.

Betty fell victim to a variation of the unrealistic thought pattern of prediction. "I should have known that if Bobby took the car, something terrible would happen to him," she told herself after her teenage son's accident. "I should never have let him borrow it." But how could Betty have known about the accident-to-be? Her son had taken the car hundreds of times before and nothing had happened. How could she possibly have predicted that he would have a serious accident this time? She couldn't. Yet she blamed herself because she hadn't foreseen it. *We cannot logically hold ourselves accountable for reasonable actions that ended in tragic consequences that we could not have foreseen.* We cannot hold ourselves accountable for our failure to predict the future.

Another manifestation of the fantasy power of prediction is the belief that we know what our lives would be like today if certain things had happened. John says, "If I had only married Sue, I would be happy now." Like Betty, John is holding himself accountable for not predicting the future (that he should have married Sue). This time, however, the failure to predict is not based on real events, such as the rise or fall of the stock market. Instead it is based on events or outcomes that never happened. John's marriage to Sue never occurred. Any imagined outcome of that "marriage" is pure speculation, especially the happy result that John now envisions as having been inevitable. In fact, a thousand different things could have destroyed the marriage to Sue or John's imagined happiness, a thousand things he could not have predicted.

The woman he now dreams of as the answer to his unhappy life might only have contributed to that unhappiness. She might have become emotionally distant. She might have spent them into bankruptcy. She might have been unfaithful. Or John might have been unfaithful to her. He might have grown to dislike her. His own unhappiness might have infected their marriage, leading them to divorce. Yet John sees only one outcome to the fantasy event of their marriage: a happiness that would have changed his life. This unrealistic thought pattern fuels his regret, a regret based solely on his imagined ability to predict what might have happened, "if only . . ."

No outcome of a fantasy event can ever be realistically assumed. The happy marriage we now imagine might have been a nightmare instead, consumed by years of fighting that produced miserable children and a bitter divorce. We can't predict that the person we didn't marry ten years ago would have made us happy today. Nor can we predict that we would be happy today if we had not squandered our money, stayed in our hometown, or pursued a different career. Future events are not predictable, and one small change in the sequence can alter everything. We cannot know what would have happened if we had taken a road other than the one we traveled. All other roads and their experiences are completely hidden from us. The future and its imagined past are never ours to know.

Are any of your regrets supported by an assumed ability to have foreseen the future?

Knowing What Others Are Thinking

If people claimed they knew what you were thinking because of their ability to read your mind, you would think them mad. Nobody can read your mind or anybody else's. Yet many of our regrets are based on the false assumption that *we* can read other people's minds—or that we should have been able to do so. The conclusions that develop from these mind-reading fantasies create regrets. We blame ourselves for things "we should have known" about others but, in fact, could not have known. Conversely, we may also blame others for things they "should have known" about us.

Earl complained, "I should have known that Joyce was thinking about leaving me." Perhaps, but perhaps not. If Joyce had never expressed her expectations, her needs, or her dissatisfaction, it would be difficult for Earl to know that she was unhappy in the relationship. Likewise, if Earl had never asked about Joyce's needs or expectations, he couldn't know what they were and that he wasn't meeting them. Neither Earl nor Joyce could read the other's mind—even though they acted as if they could.

The idea that we should know what others are thinking is highly romantic but completely unrealistic. Of course, we can often sense another's mood, but that is far different from reading his or her thoughts. The fantasy of knowing what others are thinking is often mixed with another unrealistic thought pattern: foreseeing the future. Alexis was consumed with guilt when Lana, her college-age sister, committed suicide. "I should have known she was going to kill herself," Alexis repeated over and over, implying that she should have read her sister's thoughts and predicted her actions. But it was impossible for Alexis to know of her sister's suicidal thoughts and virtually impossible to know— except in retrospect—that Lana would try to kill herself. Her sister had kept her suicidal thoughts carefully hidden, never revealing them to her older sister or alluding to them in any way.

Are any of your regrets supported by an assumption that you should have known what others were thinking or that they should have known what you were thinking?

Personalizing Events

"It's all about me." That's the assumption we make when we take everything that happens to us personally. This unrealistic thought pattern puts us at the center of things, because whatever happens to us is perceived as being about us specifically. It is not about anybody else or about fate or circumstances. It's about *us*. Other people's actions toward us are assumed to be responses *to us*, to who we are and what we are doing rather than expressions of their own individuality. Personalizing feeds our ego, of course, but it also creates a lot of discomfort and many regrets.

When we personalize, we make ourselves the cause of other people's actions that are actually taken in response to their own needs, feelings, and desires. Their actions have little or nothing to do with us, but we think they do. So we take responsibility for them. Out of that imagined responsibility, we create regrets. Personalizing generates regrets when there is nothing to regret. It convinces us that if we had just done something better or sooner, the outcome would have been different when, in fact, the outcome had virtually nothing to do with us.

Book publishers, for example, often turn down good manuscripts because they already have a similar book in production and don't want another book to cannibalize sales of their new title. Naomi, the author of a splendid nonfiction manuscript, received rejection notices from several publishers, all of whom praised her work but declined on the basis of competing books planned or published. Naomi, however, was convinced that the rejection was based on the quality of her manuscript. In other words, she thought that the rejection was about *her and her ability* rather than the result of factors unrelated to her talent. She personalized the rejection in spite of the fact that the rejection had nothing to do with the quality of her work. It was the result of a set of factors that were completely unrelated to her writing abilities. Yet Naomi deeply regrets having submitted the manuscript. "I should have polished it more," she tells herself. "Perhaps I'm not a good writer after all."

Are any of your regrets supported by having personalized someone's actions?

Incomplete Comparisons

Some of our regrets result from the comparisons we make between ourselves and others or between what we have (or don't have) and what others have. When we compare our lives to their lives, we find that our lives are lacking, and we ask ourselves what went wrong. We may try to identify what happened in our lives that prevented us from having what *they* have or what made the outcomes in our lives so different from *theirs*. Such comparisons inevitably lead to regrets, yet all such comparisons are invalid. *We don't really know what the lives of other people are like.*

We may *think* we know, but we don't know, because the data we need to judge their lives are unavailable to us. We don't know their hidden failures, secret fears, personal tragedies, or bitter regrets. Just because they *look* good doesn't mean they *feel* good. Because they *look* rich doesn't mean they *are* rich. Because they *look* happy doesn't mean they *are* happy. We have made a fundamental error of logic: an incomplete comparison based on insufficient evidence. As the expression goes, we have compared our "insides" to another person's "outsides." This comparison is always flawed.

Because we cannot read other peoples' minds, we are in no position to measure our challenges against theirs, although it seems that some people do have far greater challenges than others. And there is no question that some people seem to have far more difficult lives. Extreme poverty, severe emotional problems, incest, debilitating chronic illness, the early loss of loved ones, depression, a series of tragedies, and serious physical handicaps are all factors that make it easy for those who have experienced them to say, "My life is more difficult than so-and-so's." And perhaps it is. In making such assessments, they may well be right. But they cannot be sure.

Whatever our challenges are, we probably don't like them, but then again, we probably wouldn't like theirs either. What we do know is that no one—no matter how rich, famous, or powerful—escapes the life-shaping challenges to which we all are heir as members of the human race. Therefore we must be careful in comparing the way we feel to the way others look or appear to be. The very people we are envying may, in fact, be envying us!

Nor are such comparisons useful to us even if our lives *are* especially difficult. They only deepen our regrets and increase our sense of helplessness and hopelessness. Whatever we have experienced was ours to deal with by changing what we could and by accepting what we could not change. The facts of our lives cannot be altered, but our reactions to them can be. Whatever has happened to us has happened to us. Energy spent on bemoaning our fate is energy lost—energy that could be used to improve it or to accept it. The finite nature of human understanding precludes us from knowing all that we would like to know or even need to know to make comparisons and judgments such as these.

Are any of your regrets supported by incomplete comparisons?

Undeserved Guilt

We have all done things for which we ought to feel guilty. And we have very likely felt guilty for things we have done when little or no guilt was warranted. Guilt is an effective means of self-control, but it is also a means of controlling others. It can be used to manipulate and even ruin lives. Some parents have held their children captive for years through the power of guilt. Wives have controlled husbands, and husbands have controlled wives. Yet guilt also leads us to make amends for what we have done wrong and keeps us within our value system. It is an essential part of our makeup.

Some of us, however, have a propensity for guilt even when it isn't warranted. We seem to seek it out. Many regrets arise from such guilt, guilt that we have never examined but that originates from our unrealistic thought patterns. Perfectionism is one such thought pattern that produces guilt. The greater our need for perfection, the more likely we are to feel guilty when we fail to meet our expectations of perfection or the expectations of others.

We also take on undeserved guilt when we have an unreasonable desire to please people. When conflicting demands are made on us that we cannot meet, we have no reason to feel guilty when we reject one or more of them. But instead of saying no, disappointing someone, and letting it go, we feel guilty for not having pleased everyone. The guilt isn't warranted.

As with the other unrealistic thought patterns, we may also use guilt to avoid accepting responsibility for our lives. We do so when we don't work to make our lives better, because we "don't deserve it."

With an unrealistic commitment to perfection, an exaggerated need to please others, or a desire to avoid responsibility, we become putty in the hands of those who would use guilt to exploit us. We have to distinguish between a legitimate criticism or a legitimate analysis of our actions and one that is simply wrong or motivated by hidden agendas. Whenever we accept the criticism of others without weighing its merits, we are turning our power to analyze and evaluate over to someone else. Not every criticism is valid, and not every source of criticism is reliable or trustworthy. We do not have to accept guilt imposed by anyone else. Nor should we accept guilt without a careful analysis that involves our confidant and other trusted sources of good counsel.

We can defend ourselves from unwarranted guilt, because guilt results from actions that can be identified and analyzed. The manufactured guilt that we create or the exaggerated guilt that we take on from others can be rejected through thought analysis. Thought analysis will establish the validity or invalidity of any guilt we feel. Such analysis is tricky, however. We can delude ourselves into believing that we have done nothing wrong, just as we can uncritically accept the warranted guilt that we or others try to place on us.

Working with our confidant, we can determine whether the guilt we feel is merited. We can determine whether it comes from living or long-dead parents, from outmoded ideas, or from unrealistic thought patterns. Beyond such thought analysis, we can journal, pray, and meditate about the incident that created the guilt and our role in it. While we must never shirk our moral responsibilities, neither should we take on those that are not ours. Manufactured guilt can be recognized and rejected. Real guilt can be released through the Ten Steps.

Are any of your regrets supported by undeserved guilt?

Reimagining the Past

Reimagining the past is a thought pattern we use to create regrets when we fondly remember what never was and then compare it to the way things are now. In reimagining, we return to the past to exaggerate the good while forgetting the bad. Through selective forgetting of some events and selective enhancement of others, reimagining leads us to the erroneous conclusion that whatever we have now is not nearly as good as what we used to have. Ricardo compares his present job to an "ideal" job he once had, forgetting how much he disliked his boss, how difficult the commute was, and how happy he was to escape. Now he regrets leaving the old job. But the regret is manufactured. Ricardo couldn't wait to leave that job.

Regina remembers a failed affair as a storybook romance, forgetting the fights, the betrayals, and the afternoons spent crying. She regrets not marrying the former love object whom she came to reject, thinking now that their relationship would have matured after their marriage and the great things about him would have overshadowed the weaknesses that seemed so glaring at the time. By remembering only the good, forgetting most of the bad, and making a false comparison between the past and the present, Regina is reimagining the past.

A reimagined past, like any fantasy comparison, leads us to false conclusions that create or intensify our regrets. In some cases, letting go of a regret means letting go of the reimagined past that created it. Fortunately, thought analysis and the other spiritual and psychological tools are effective in reminding us of what things were really like and helping us let go of the selective forgetting and selective enhancements on which our reimagined past is built.

Another way to reimagine the past is to relive it—but with different choices. We go back to the past and make different decisions about our career, the way we spent our time, the goals we pursued, or any number of other factors. We imagine, for example, that we had gone into teaching instead of law, that we had spent less time at the office and more time with our family, that we had devoted ourselves to enriching people's lives rather than earning money to buy material things. We change the choices we made and imagine the happy life we would have led "if only" we had chosen differently.

Sometimes the reimagined past was not even possible but not having it is regretted nonetheless. Paul, for example, has a hugely successful career, an enormous home in the most prestigious part of the city, high-achieving children, an enviable social life, and many friends in the corridors of power through which he moves with ease and authority. Yet he has a deep and abiding regret that torments him. He didn't go to an Ivy League college. Many of his friends did. Oh, he went to a good state school, but it's not the same to him. Not the same as having gone to Harvard, the focus of his regret. He didn't apply to Harvard because when he was eighteen, it never occurred to him to do so. Now he realizes what he missed—or thinks he missed. Paul sent two children to Harvard, but *he* didn't go. Now it's too late. He'll never have an Ivy League education, he'll never be *one of them*. Paul suffers from a reimagined past, a past that could not possibly have been. Yet it is a past that poisons his present. Rather than focusing on the gifts of his life, including those that came from the state university he attended, Paul is focused on the one thing that he does not have—the one thing that keeps everything from being perfect.

Many of the good things in life are mutually exclusive, equally attractive in different ways, and not easy to choose among. Life is made up of many forks in the road, forks that diverge. We can have one alternative, but we cannot have both. We cannot have the presence of our family and long hours at work, for example. We cannot enjoy the single life and get married. We cannot spend money and save that money at the same time. We have to choose. Potential regrets lie with either choice. So do potential rewards.

Everything in life competes for the limited amount of time we have. Every choice for something is a choice against something else. Choosing one career generally means abandoning another, at least for awhile. Ironically, the more successful we are, the more significant the nature and number of mutually exclusive choices we have to make, the greater the number of opportunities we must turn down, and the more attractive those lost opportunities are. Therefore, the more successful and rich our lives, the more we can potentially regret. Each choice between mutually exclusive alternatives produces regrets. But to live in regret is a choice, too.

Are any of your regrets supported by reimagining the past?

Extreme Thinking

Extreme thinking is an all-or-nothing, black-and-white thought pattern. With extreme thinking, it's everything or nothing. There is no second, third, or fourth place and no second, third, or fourth chance—only first place or failure. Extreme thinking takes us out of the reality of a complex and nuanced world and carries us to a simplistic world devoid of contradictions, paradox, and ambiguity. It's a guaranteed formula for creating and maintaining regrets.

Alejandro has a core regret that fuels many others: he never finished college. "I should have done it ten years ago," he says, "when I had the chance. But I didn't. Now it's too late. It'll never happen. I'll never have the opportunities I could have had." Alejandro is thirty-five. Even if he were seventy-five, it would not be too late to get a college degree. It's only too late for Alejandro because he sees no second chance. Extreme thinking has severely limited his options. It also maintains his regret and keeps him from doing something about the problem he claims is at the root of his troubles: no college degree. It justifies his inaction.

With extreme thinking, our failure is total when we make a mistake or miss an opportunity. With no second chance, we have no way to correct our errors, no way out of our problems. We are trapped. When Chen's girlfriend broke up with him, he told himself and others, "I'll never get married now." Such all-or-nothing thinking deepens and prolongs the regrets we hold. In Chen's case, that unrealistic thought pattern made his regret over the breakup much worse—and more desperate. In addition to making regrets more severe, all-or-nothing thinking can create new regrets as well—regrets of omission—if it prevents us from trying again, from taking advantage of the second chance.

When everything is perceived as black and white, all-or-nothing, there is little room for forgiveness or compassion. We miss the nuances of our options, the subtleties of our opportunities, and the complexities of our decisions that explain our mistakes or offer us another chance. We are sadly shortchanged by what we think cannot be altered or can never happen.

Which, if any, of your regrets are supported by extreme thinking?

Using Regrets as Justification for Inaction

Certain thought patterns, carried to an extreme, provide the excuse we're looking for to avoid taking action to improve our lives. "If only such-and-such had happened," we tell ourselves and others, we wouldn't have to: go back to college, start dating again, find another job, quit smoking, restrict our spending, or do countless other things that we don't want to do. Instead of taking action, we lament the past. Whatever change is required, we tell ourselves, can't be made now because it had to have been made *then,* at the time of the regret. We claim that we are too old for college, that we don't have the time with a family and a job, or that we can't afford it. Rather than seek a second job to get us out of debt, we complain that we are overqualified for the part-time jobs available or that we shouldn't have to take such a job, and that we wouldn't have to, "if only . . ."

The justifications we use for inaction excuse our failure to exert the effort, exercise the discipline, or overcome the fear that the achievement of our goals demands. These justifications fuel our fantasy that "if only" things had been different, we would be happier and more successful than we are today. We are confident, for example, that "If only I had been born with as much money as my cousin, I would be as successful." Perhaps, and perhaps not. It is painful to admit that we might not have been as successful as our point of comparison *even if* we had been born with as much money. Or that we might not have a better job *even if* we had gone to college. Or that the marriage that failed was not our spouse's fault but ours (or ours as well). Or that regardless of what happened in the past, we would still find ourselves having to address the present and the challenges it brings.

The suffering we endure from holding onto our regrets through inaction is far greater than the suffering we would experience in letting them go and facing the reality of the present with all of its challenges, opportunities, and potentiality. Yet the seductive "benefit" of doing nothing calls to us, suggesting that it is more comfortable to give into the past and its failures than to act in the present, with all its promises. In the dreamy, do-nothing world of regretting, we can be confident that everything would have worked out, *if only . . .*

Two forms of toxic thought patterns that are often used as justification for inaction are habitual complaining and playing the role of the perpetual victim.

HABITUAL COMPLAINING

Some of us have raised complaining to an art. It is the primary focus of our conversations and the center of our lives. Regrets that we can link to life's injustices, to destructive behavior aimed at us, or to unfair deprivations we've had to endure give us something to complain about regularly, whether to ourselves or to others. Perhaps we hold an infantile hope that if we complain enough, our "parents" (in whatever form) will relieve our complaints and make us happy. Then we won't have to accept that responsibility for ourselves. Or perhaps we enjoy making others unhappy as a sign of our power, or perhaps focusing every conversation on us and our regrets satisfies our self-centeredness. To give up our regrets would mean giving up our complaints and hence the way we relate to the world. It isn't easy to stop complaining about the past when such complaining has become a way of life. But it is possible.

Jenny is an example of a chronic complainer. She complains to herself, to her friends, and to her children about many things. But her chief complaint is her ex-husband, whom she blames for her present unhappiness and the desperate financial condition she faces. If only he hadn't divorced her, she tells herself and those who will listen, if only he had left her well off financially, or if only he had made it possible for her to earn a decent living. This regret of her failed marriage is the centerpiece of her life. It brings her some measure of sympathy, gives her energy when she gets angry about it, and allows her to complain bitterly about life's injustices and the viciousness of her ex-husband. Her constant complaining also substitutes for action—for doing something to improve her situation, such as increasing her earning capacity or changing a negative attitude that drives people away. Jenny's habitual complaining and the inaction it seems to justify keep her tied to her regrets. She remains focused on the past, which she is helpless to change, instead of living in the present where change is still possible.

PERPETUAL VICTIM

True victims beset by tragedy and deep suffering elicit our well-deserved sympathy. Some of us, however, are addicted to sympathy, whether deserved or not, and to the attention it brings. So we turn ourselves into victims of past events, living in our regrets instead of the present, and filled with a cloying self-pity about the regrets of our lives. Regrets of a certain kind allow us to be impressive, woe-filled victims who wallow in easy attention, others' sympathy, and an irresponsibility that we justify to ourselves. In that role, we are great people who would have achieved great things and been wildly happy if only such-and-such had happened—or hadn't happened.

We may position ourselves as self-righteous martyrs suffering at the hands of wicked people, an unjust fate, or terrible circumstances, subtly or aggressively recounting our tales of woe to all who will listen, including ourselves. Some of us take a different tack, presenting ourselves as saints who have gallantly endured an endless string of horrors we are only too happy to recount. Or perhaps we choose to be brave survivors of terrible events that we continuously revisit—and never let go. All of these victim roles rely on regrets to legitimize our victim status. To let go of our regrets would mean having to learn a new role, to become something other than life's victim. It would mean having to take responsibility for our lives. It would mean having to do something about them in the present.

2. Use Thought Analysis to Counter Toxic Thoughts That Support the Regret

Although you may have experienced toxic thought patterns for years, it is not necessary to continue being hurt by them. You can counteract toxic thoughts and reduce their occurrence by challenging them through thought analysis whenever they crop up. The process of using thought analysis to identify and counteract toxic thought patterns that support your regrets consists of four steps:

1. Listen critically to the thoughts you have about your regrets. What is it that you tell yourself about them?
2. Identify the thoughts related to your regrets that arise from toxic thought patterns, such as perfectionism, exaggerated control, or justification for inaction.
3. Analyze the validity of the thought by asking yourself such questions as, "Is this statement true?" "Is it fair?" "Is it realistic?" Ask yourself if you are really expected to be perfect, to predict the future, or to know what others are thinking.
4. Act on your analysis by rejecting the thought if it is invalid (unfair, untrue, or unrealistic). Tell yourself that the toxic thought is false and that you reject it. You do not have to be convinced, swayed, or influenced by thoughts that can't stand up to the scrutiny of thought analysis. Tell yourself that the toxic thought is an old thought that you no longer entertain and that no longer has power over you. See yourself letting it go, releasing it into the air like a balloon that floats away.

Generally, toxic thoughts begin with some variation of "I should have" or "If only I had." When such thoughts arise, ask yourself if they are really true. Could you or should you *really* have done such-and-such at the time? Do the "should haves" and "could haves" through which you blame yourself arise from perfectionism, a sense of exaggerated control, or foreseeing the future? Do they come from incomplete comparisons, reimagining the past, personalizing events, or some other toxic thought pattern?

The use of thought analysis to counter toxic thought patterns is a process that requires continuous practice. The thought habits of a lifetime are not quickly changed, but they can be countered, neutralized, and gradually altered though persistent work. Progress, not perfection, is the goal with this step.

Step Three has been worked when you have identified the toxic thought patterns that support your regrets and have committed to countering them in your daily life.

7

STEP FOUR: GRIEVING LOSSES

GRIEF IS PART of all regretting. In fact, the word *regret* has its origins in the Middle English word *regrete,* meaning to lament or to feel sorrow and, before that, in the Old English word *graetan,* meaning to weep. Antecedents to regret also appear in Old French as *regreter,* meaning to long after, to bewail, or to lament someone's death, and in the Old Norse word *grata,* meaning to weep or moan. Sorrow, sadness, longing, and grief are such a part of our regrets that the very word means to grieve.

This step acknowledges the legitimate suffering we have endured because of our regrets and allows us to fully and properly grieve our hurt, whatever it is. If we lost a loved one physically through death or emotionally through illness or incapacitation, we feel how deeply that loss has affected us. If we created a scandal, we feel the anguish it caused us and those we love. If we intentionally hurt our spouse in an ugly divorce, we grieve the pain that our cruelty caused.

But Step Four also limits the period of suffering that we must endure. Although we will feel the sadness of our loss as intensely as we need to feel it, we also recognize that our grief was meant to be a temporary means of healing and not a permanent agony. This step acknowledges the pain of our loss even as it helps us put that loss behind us.

In earlier centuries, a specific period of time was set aside for mourning the death of a loved one. During the mourning period, which was usually a year, the bereaved were expected to experience the terrible pain of their loss, accept the love and support of their friends, and make peace with the change in their lives. After the mourning period was up, however, the bereaved were expected to bring their grief to an end and resume an involved, productive, and ultimately happy life.

The Nature of Losses

Losses in life are inevitable. They are built into life, including both its successes and its failures. Some losses are sudden and obvious: termination from a job we liked, a house that burned, a parent who died. Some are slow and subtle: the loss of youth, vitality, or the possibility of pursuing a career in a certain field. Other losses are buried in gains, so we don't see them as losses at first: moving out of our parents' house, graduating from college, changing cities for a better job. All of these gains entail losses—losses that we willingly give up for the gains we achieve, but they are losses nonetheless. Other losses are intellectual, such as the realization that we have been wrong about a cherished belief that we have held for many years. Losses may be spiritual, such as the shattering loss of the belief in a loving God.

Still other "losses" are not really losses at all because we never had them in the first place. Yet they feel like real losses and, in a sense, they are. These losses may be the hopes and dreams we once had for ourselves that can no longer be achieved, basic needs that went unmet, or fundamental expectations that were never satisfied: a nurturing family, enough to eat, a safe neighborhood, or parents who lived beyond our childhood. These losses are as real in our regrets as the losses of people and things we once experienced.

Grieving Losses

Every loss brings pain and grief. When the losses are great, the pain is great. We have three different options regarding the losses of our regrets, but only one of these options leads to healing. The first option is to refuse to revisit the losses and feel their sadness, thus sacrificing our only means of healing the suffering they cause. The second option is to feel the pain of our regrets but never bring that pain to an end, creating continuous or intermittent states of suffering. The third alternative is to return to the regret and its pain in a structured way in order to feel that pain, express it, accept it, make peace with it, and let it go. Achieving the third option is the purpose of this step.

Grief brings healing, and the only way to healing is through grief. There is no way around it, only through it. If we refuse to grieve or if we don't know how to grieve, we will continue to suffer as long as we live. Because regrets always involve losses and because losses always involve pain, we have to work through the pain of those losses and let it go, or we cannot let go of our regrets.

In her landmark book *On Death and Dying*, Elisabeth Kübler-Ross, M.D., described the five stages through which all dying patients journey in coming to terms with their own deaths: shock and denial, anger, bargaining, sadness, and acceptance. Understanding these stages is helpful to anyone dealing with significant loss, even if the loss is emotional or spiritual rather than physical. Every loss, after all, is a form of death, whether it is the loss of a job or the loss of a dream. Both physical and psychological losses can mean the end of relationships, interaction, and experiences. Like the death of a loved one, the death of things that are important to us (the death of youth, of a career, of a promising future) must be grieved and accepted. Although we feel these losses in the emotional realm, they are as real as the losses we feel in the physical realm. Like a broken bone, they must be treated carefully and with patience if they are to heal properly.

The five-stage process through which the dying find acceptance of their loss is described in the following paragraphs. Acceptance is not inevitable, however. It is possible to remain fixed in any one of the stages just as it is possible to be working on more than one of them simultaneously.

Stage I: Shock and Denial

The initial reaction to loss is temporary: a state of shock from which we gradually recover. When the protective numbness of the shock wears off, we replace it immediately with something else: denial. In the face of ir-refutable evidence, we refuse to accept the truth of our loss by denying it. "No, it can't be happening," we say, "It can't be true," "I'm sure that's not right," "There must be some mistake." Shock and denial are temporary re-sponses that provide the time we need to marshal our intellectual, psycho-logical, and spiritual resources to deal with the crisis of serious loss.

Stage 2: Anger

Once shock and denial fade, we experience anger and even rage. "Why me?" we demand. We direct our anger at anyone, scattershot style. We may focus it on the loved one who died, on the doctors who attended her, or on the spouse who didn't somehow prevent her death. Our anger can be directed at God, at fate, or at the unfairness of life. It can manifest as rage, as envy of those who still have what we lost, or as a resentment at those who have escaped a similar loss.

But anger provides no real relief from grief. So without consciously thinking about it, we adopt a different approach, one designed to erase the loss, to take it away as if it had never happened. Like a small child whose temper tantrum has not yielded the results he wants, we take a more con-ciliatory tack. We try bargaining.

Stage 3: Bargaining

The bargaining stage is brief but significant. It is the "if only" moment in which we try to bargain with God, fate, or whatever we believe in that might be able to make things different or to protect us from the loss. Like frightened children, we promise to be good for the rest of our lives, to change our ways, to do anything if only our loss isn't true or its conse-quences don't happen. Perhaps we magically try to eliminate or reduce the loss by reliving our regret over and over—but with the results we want—asking ourselves again and again why it couldn't have turned out that way. This futile rumination is one last attempt to hold at bay the unacceptable reality of our loss and the terrible pain that will accompany it.

Stage 4: Sadness

When numbness wears off, denial fails, anger abates, and bargaining is perceived as futile, a terrible sense of loss comes over us. We feel profoundly sad, depressed, and dispirited. This is the stage of depression, the time of grieving, in which we lament what we have lost, feel the pain of that loss, and express our sorrow openly. In this stage of healing, we are immersed in pain, abandoning the stiff upper lip, ignoring the suggestions to cheer up. We feel the loss beyond measure. These are the times when we cry, when the choking sobs and the streaming tears cleanse us of the pain and sorrow. As we return to the regret to grieve it, even many years after it occurred, we reencounter the sadness of the regret itself and all the intervening years. This moment is the darkest of the night, the bleakest period before the dawn.

Stage 5: Acceptance

As we hurt, we are healing, bringing the sadness of the depression stage to an end. When we have expressed the sadness we feel, we begin to accept that we cannot change what has happened. We are no longer angry or depressed about the regret and its consequences. Our deep sadness has been grieved away. We have found acceptance. That does not mean that we will never again feel sad about our regret, but it does mean that we can manage that sadness, that we can come to terms with it so that it does not torment us. We have removed another barrier to accepting our regret as part of our life and letting it go.

Acceptance means that we no longer resist reality but give into it where our regret is concerned. We acknowledge that we cannot fight the inevitable. We agree to live life on life's terms rather than demanding that life meet our terms. We recognize that true healing comes from accepting what we cannot change. Acceptance is a recognition that we are called to make the best of things, even when they are not to our liking. It is an act of wisdom and power, not of defeat and weakness, because it comes out of our humility and our courage. Acceptance is an acknowledgment that we are not the ultimate power in the universe and cannot always have our own way, no matter how much it hurts.

Working Step Four

Step Four consists of two Action List items. The first is a journaling exercise that identifies and describes the losses you need to grieve. The second is to return to the pain of those losses in order to grieve them and pass through that grief on the way to acceptance. If you have truly grieved your losses, this step will not be necessary.

The Action List for Step Four is shown below:

Action List: Step Four

Grieving Losses

1. Describe the losses of your regrets
2. Grieve your losses

I. Describe the Losses of Your Regrets

For each regret, describe the losses that you have suffered and need to grieve. These losses may have resulted from your own actions or from the actions of others, from events over which you had no control, or from ill-fated circumstances. Perhaps they are the result of comparisons between your present life and what might have been. Many of these losses have already been described in your journaling activities from previous steps. Frank regretted his overspending and the emotional problems with which he had struggled. He had to grieve the deprivations he had created for his family, particularly in comparison to his friends, who drove reliable cars, took long vacations, wore new clothes, sent their children to better schools, and enjoyed the promise of an early retirement.

Your own regrets may be based on something that you missed through no fault of your own, such as loving parents. Perhaps you were physically or emotionally abused as a child, one of your parents abandoned you at an early age, or your parents were cruel or rejecting. Perhaps they were alcoholics or drug addicts or terribly poor or kept you from pursuing the career you desperately wanted. Perhaps they never gave you the support you needed, the education life demanded, or the upbringing you coveted. Perhaps you suffered from bad health, a physical impairment, or an emotional problem that cost you dearly, made you different from others, or restricted your potential.

Whatever the painful losses of your regrets may be, describe them in this journal entry. These are the losses you will grieve.

2. Grieve Your Losses

If you have not grieved the losses of your regret, begin by asking yourself which stage of grief you are in with this regret. When you have identified the stage, work on moving to the next stage. For example, if you are trapped in anger, work to give up the anger by opening yourself to the pain that lies beneath it. If you are in bargaining, work to accept that nothing you can do now will change the facts of your regret. If you are in grief, open yourself to that grief, to feeling the pain of your loss.

Use the spiritual and psychological tools to help you progress through the stages of grief. Pray for the courage to recognize that the events of the regret cannot be changed, to feel the pain of what happened, to find acceptance. Journal about your pain, your fear, your terrible sadness. Reveal how deeply it has hurt, how hard it has been to bear, how much you wanted it to be different. Journal about accepting what you cannot change, about looking for acceptance. Visualize yourself grieving and bringing that grief to an end, finding acceptance and release from the pain. Affirm, "I feel the pain of my regret," "I accept the losses I have sustained," "I am willing to grieve," or "I am bringing my grief to an end."

Grief should not go on forever. So even as you grieve, recognize that one day you will release this pain. Begin to feel the cleansing of the soul that the tears and sadness bring. This time, the grieving over your regrets is not random or sporadic but purposeful. It is not a sudden shot of pain from out of the blue nor a slow ache that comes from nowhere. It is pain resurrected and managed for a purpose. And it is not pain to which you must ever return again with this intensity. Even having completed Step Four, you may still have sadness about your regrets. The loss of a loved one, for example, is something that, to some degree, never stops hurting. Yet the grief that interferes with letting go of your regret can be released and acceptance of the loss can be found. We may grieve our losses many times in working the steps, but now, at least, we have exposed our grief and know that it is manageable.

With the completion of Step Four, you are ready for the next step. It will take you from the pain of your regrets to the healing process of making amends.

8

STEP FIVE: MAKING AMENDS

SOME REGRETS BRING a heavy burden of guilt. The guilt may stem from our acts of commission or omission toward others, or it may result from what we have done to ourselves. Step Five addresses this oppressive aspect of many regrets: a deep sense of guilt. Regret-based guilt can be intense and debilitating. It erodes our self-worth and corrodes our happiness. Like resentments, it binds us to the past and ties us to our regrets. Letting go of the guilt is part of letting go of the regret.

Not every regret results in guilt, of course. When regrets arise entirely from circumstances beyond our control (such as a physical impairment) or from the actions of others (such as childhood abuse), we are not likely to feel guilty. But we might. Children often feel guilty about parental abuse, because they erroneously believe they deserve it. And even when we didn't cause a regret, we sometimes wrestle with the vague feeling that we are somehow responsible, that in some unknown way we should have done better.

If you have no guilt from your regrets and you have hurt no one, you do not need to work Step Five. The objective of Step Five is to make amends to the people you've harmed as a result of your regrets. If you have harmed no one, you have nothing for which to make an amend.

Most regrets are not guiltless, however. Even if you played no role in creating your regret, you may have hurt others by harboring it. You have certainly hurt yourself, and so you need to make an amend for that harm, which is a self-amend. But you may have hurt others as well. Larry, for example, has never forgiven his father for the beatings he received as a child and a young adolescent. Larry's anger over that abuse has poisoned his relationship with his siblings, because he insists on denouncing his father whenever they talk, even though they no longer wish to hear it. The resulting estrangement is painful for Larry's siblings, who have been hurt by Larry's failure to let go of his regret.

Step Five uses an established psychological and spiritual principle for releasing guilt: accepting accountability and making amends. By accepting responsibility for whatever part you played in creating your regrets and by making amends to the people you have harmed, you will be freed from whatever guilt the regret has brought. Ironically, only by acknowledging accountability can you find release from the pain of that accountability. Although in this step you are going to reexamine what you have done wrong, your purpose is not to heap more blame on yourself. Nor is it to make you feel worse than you already do about what you have done. Instead, it is to make you feel better. Only by identifying your wrongful actions and making amends for them can you release the guilt that ties you to the past.

To acknowledge personal accountability is a courageous act. You may be tempted to avoid the necessary self-examination, the admission of guilt, and the making of amends. If you overcome this temptation and complete Step Five, you will find the freedom from guilt that you seek. And you will have moved one step closer to letting go of your regrets.

Working Step Five

Our Action List for Step Five consists of three activities:

Action List: Step Five

Making Amends

1. Determine the appropriate amends for the request
2. Make the apology and reparations
3. Change the harmful behavior

Each of these activities assumes that you have identified the part you played in your regrets and can describe the actions you took or didn't take that hurt other people. That's a fair assumption to make, because in Step Two you did, in fact, examine your regrets in detail, describe your role in them, and list the people you hurt. You may want to refer back to Step Two in your journal before continuing with this step.

When the first two activities on the Action List have been accomplished, you will have completed the step in the sense that you will be ready to move to Step Six. The third activity of changing your behavior is ongoing, and it may be something that you will have to work on for a lifetime. But there's no reason to be discouraged by that prospect. After all, that's what lifetimes are for.

Now, let's examine each of the activities.

1. Determine the Appropriate Amends for the Request

To amend something is to change it. Usually, the change corrects a problem or a deficiency. The amends we make in Step Five are designed to correct the problems that we created with our regrets. They are our attempt to repair, to the best of our ability, the hurt and damage we caused. An amend is a complex activity that consists of three components. Each of the components is necessary or the amend will be incomplete. The three components are: an apology, reparation for damages, and changed behavior. Since there is often confusion about the difference among these components (and even surprise about some of them), it's worth it to have a closer look at each.

Apology

An apology is the starting point of every amend. Through our apology, we:

1. Acknowledge our inappropriate behavior (what we did wrong).
2. Accept responsibility for that inappropriate behavior.
3. Hold ourselves accountable for the negative consequences of that behavior.

4. Express sorrow for what we have done wrong.
5. Assure the other person that we won't do it again.
6. Seek pardon from the injured party (which we may not get, of
    course. If we don't, it's okay for reasons that will be explained in
    chapter 12).

An apology sounds complicated and involved, but it isn't. In fact, it
comes quite naturally. For example, a simple but complete apology from
an adolescent boy to his father might be something like, "Dad, I'm sorry
(expressing sorrow for what he did wrong) about the damage (the negative
consequence) I just caused (accepting accountability) when I backed into
the garage (the inappropriate behavior) and knocked the wall out (negative consequence). I hope you'll forgive me (seeking pardon) and not
ground me forever (seeking more pardon). I promise I'll be more careful
next time and won't do it again (assurance of nonrepetition and of a future
change in behavior)."

An apology is the first step in making an amend, because it acknowledges our inappropriate behavior, but it is only the first step. We also have
to make reparations.

Reparations

A reparation is an attempt to repair something. In making amends, the
purpose of a reparation is to repair as much as we can of the damage we
caused. Ideally the goal is to achieve a complete restoration to the preregret
condition. But a complete restoration is seldom possible, especially in relationships and in other complicated situations. So realistically we do the
best we can. We try to repair as much of the damage as possible, given the
limitations imposed by the circumstances of the regret.

In the example of the teenage boy who backed into the garage, the issue
of reparations is relatively straightforward. Or is it? Ideally he would offer
to pay for the damage to the garage, restoring it to its condition before
the accident. That would be a perfect reparation. Except that, of course, he
may not have the money to do it and, depending upon the extent of the
damage, may not be able to earn it. Or perhaps his parents don't think it's

in his best interests to have to earn it because of other demands on his time, such as high school. Perhaps they'll ask him to pay a portion of the costs. But what portion? And over what period of time? Or perhaps they'll decide that it was an accident and that an apology and a promise to be more careful next time (changed behavior) is sufficient. In that case, there would be no reparation component to his amend.

Those reparations that involve physical damage, stolen funds, or anything else in which most of the harm can be quantified would seem to be relatively straightforward. But even they grow complicated in real life. Tony, for example, embezzled from his company but was never caught. Eaten away by guilt, he came to regret his theft and wanted to make amends in order to be free of that guilt. What should his reparations be and how should he make them? Tony and his confidant decided that the most effective reparation for all concerned would be for him to repay the money he stole, plus interest. But how should he make that repayment? Should he reveal his embezzlement and face a possible jail sentence as part of his reparations? Or should he repay the money anonymously? If he doesn't have all the money, should he pay it in installments? Should he take a second job to pay it back more quickly? If his company has gone out of business, to whom should he pay the money he stole? The answers to these questions depend upon Tony and the nature of the unique circumstances surrounding his regret.

What about reparations for people who are deceased or unreachable? They can still be made. Ramón had failed to repay a five-thousand-dollar loan from a good friend with whom a dispute erupted that grew and grew until it destroyed their friendship. When the man died, Ramón began to deeply regret the dispute and the end of the friendship that had once meant so much to him. He also regretted not repaying the debt. In this case, he was able to repay it to his friend's widow. But what if his friend had no widow or the widow could not be located? In that case, Ramón could have made reparations by donating five thousand dollars (plus interest) to the heirs of the estate or to a worthy charity.

When a reparation involves human relationships, it grows even more complicated—and even more interesting. The choice of reparations is a complex decision that requires a great deal of thought, contemplation, and prayer. It is easy to make a mistake by acting prematurely or without having thought through the reparation and its possible consequences. For that reason, turn to your confidant for help *before* you take any action. Your confidant should play a critical role in helping you choose the reparations you intend to make. He or she will ensure the most productive reparation possible while protecting the interests of every party to the regret, including yours. A confidant is your defense against ill-advised acts that might injure you, other people associated with the regret, or innocent third parties.

A confidant is there to guide you as well as protect you. A confidant's perspective is likely to be more objective and disciplined than yours and perhaps more creative in resolving the potentially complicated issues associated with making reparations. A confidant will prevent you from being too easy on yourself and, conversely, from being too hard in the reparations you choose. As your supportive partner, he or she will establish guidelines to keep you safe and deadlines to keep you moving.

In designing your amend (apology, reparations, and changed behavior), keep in mind that there are two major criteria that should be met: effectiveness and no further harm.

EFFECTIVENESS

The first criterion to apply in selecting an amend, including its reparations, is *effectiveness*. An amend should right the wrong you committed as completely as possible, generally without regard to its consequences for you. If you want freedom from your regrets, you cannot buy it with half-measures. Your apology, reparations, and changed behavior must be the best you can manage given present circumstances. Only if you are thorough in designing and making your amends will they prove entirely satisfactory to you. In that case, they will cleanse you of the guilt you feel and restore you to a sense of worth and wellness. The reparation component does not have to be complete in the sense of restoring everything to its pre-regret state, which isn't possible, but it should be complete enough to restore you to freedom.

With some regrets, there may be no reparations to make. In relationships, especially, there may be no way to repair what has happened other than with an apology and a change in your behavior. If so, then Step Five has only the apology and behavioral change components to it, but you must have given serious consideration to reparations and whether they were possible or appropriate.

NO FURTHER HARM

The second criterion by which to judge the effectiveness of an amend is whether it can cause further harm to the injured party or to an innocent third party. You have no right to make an amend that assuages your guilty conscience if it harms someone else. Such an act is not an amend but an indulgence. The defining test for an appropriate amend is whether the other person will be better off or worse off after the amend has been made. For example, should Collin reveal to his wife a deeply regretted, short-lived extramarital affair when she knows nothing of it? That is a difficult question to answer unless unsafe sex was involved, which poses a health risk that must be addressed. Otherwise, careful thought should be given to the nature of the amend and to whether an apology should be made that reveals the affair.

Many marriages end when an extramarital affair is divulged. So what would be Collin's best course of action for everyone involved? The answer depends on his situation. Do he and his wife have children, for example? Is their marriage strong enough to handle the infidelity or will the revelation inevitably lead to divorce? Will the guilt of Collin's unrevealed regret drive an emotional wedge between him and his wife? These are difficult questions to answer. An apology (an acceptance of responsibility and expression of regret) may not be appropriate in this case if it will destroy the marriage and imperil his children's future. Regardless of how guilty Collin feels and how much he would like to get rid of that guilt, he cannot do it in a manner that will hurt his wife or his children.

Tony's embezzlement case provides another illustration of how careful you have to be in making amends. If repaying the stolen funds directly to his former company would bring a jail sentence and deprive Tony's small children of their only source of livelihood, it would not be his best choice. Perhaps, instead, Tony's repayment should be made anonymously.

Whatever he decides, Tony's reparation will have to meet the second criterion for an effective amend: no further harm to anyone else.

2. Make the Apology and Reparations

Once you have decided on the nature of your amends, the second part of Step Five is to make the apology and the reparations. Making the apology itself may not be easy, emotionally or otherwise. Some of the people to whom you want to make amends, for example, may no longer be living. How do you make apologies and reparations to the deceased? Some of the people on your amends list will be willing to talk with you, but others will not be. How do you apologize to them? Some apologies should be made in person, but that may not be possible. Other apologies will be better made by telephone or by mail. Apologies to people you hate or to people who have hurt you more than you have hurt them are particularly difficult.

Overcoming Resistance to the Difficult Apology

Some apologies seem quite natural to us and are relatively easy to make. Some we actually *want* to make. We feel guilty, we love the person we've hurt, we are sorry, and we will do anything we can to make things right. Wrecking a spouse's car is one such example. These are the easy apologies, relatively speaking. The difficult apologies are the ones that we don't want to make or those that we can't make through normal communication channels because the other person is deceased or irrational. Regardless of how difficult our apology is, however, we have to make it. We can't get around these amends. As a result, we have to resist a natural inclination not to apologize to those who have hurt us or to make such apologies only after the offending parties have made their apologies first. The problem with waiting for other people to act is that they may never go first. It might happen, but why bet our happiness on it?

One way to overcome our resistance to apologizing is to understand why we make amends. We do so to free ourselves of guilt and so of our regrets. We make amends to others, *regardless of what they have done to us*, because *we make the amends for our benefit,* not for theirs. Therefore, *what other people have done to us is irrelevant as long as we owe them an amend.* This idea is contrary to the way people usually think about amends. Generally we think of amends as something we do *for* somebody else. Some amends, of course, we do make for the benefit of others, such as to a child we love and have inadvertently hurt or a spouse with whom we want to maintain good relations. But the reason we make amends *for our regrets* is to help us get rid of those regrets.

The idea that we make amends primarily for ourselves rather than others sounds selfish, but it isn't. We have a right and a responsibility to take care of ourselves, to grow spiritually and psychologically, and so we have a need to make amends *for ourselves* when they are warranted. We make these amends to get right with ourselves, with our higher power, and with the parties we have hurt. There are other reasons for making amends, such as being the morally right thing to do, but the practical effect of making an amend is that it rids us of the guilt that ties us to our regrets.

Even if the other party has hurt us more than we have hurt her and even if she won't admit to hurting us at all, we still apologize for whatever we have done. We make that apology because we played a role in the regret, and making it is what we have to do to let go of that regret. What the other parties do about their part in the regret, if anything, is up to them. It is not up to us. They must find their own peace as best they can.

Using the Spiritual and Psychological Tools to Overcome Resistance

The spiritual and psychological tools are powerful resources that will help you with this difficult step. They can be used before beginning the step and for all step activities. For example, pray for the strength and courage to overcome resistance to working the step, to be honest with yourself in confronting the harm you have caused, and to be resourceful in designing your reparations. Ask your higher power for the discipline and patience you need to make your apologies, that others will be receptive to hearing them, and that you will handle yourself with compassion and restraint. Ask your higher power to help you make reparations, to change your behavior as part of your amend, and to help you find freedom from the guilt and shame of these regrets.

Creative visualizations will be effective in reducing your fear level and moving you through this step. Visualize yourself making apologies to each of the people you will approach, being well received by them, and leaving grateful that you talked with them. When the recipient of the amend is deceased or unreachable, use creative visualization to enrich the power of the healing letter you write. See the recipient reading the letter, being grateful for having received it, and forgiving you for all of your past actions.

If the fear and pain of determining the appropriate reparations and then making them proves overwhelming, journal about those feelings. Write about the need for the amends, the fears you have about making them, the worst the other party could do to hurt you, and the resources you have available to support and encourage you. Write about your reluctance, your sadness, and your fear. Encourage yourself in your journal by reminding yourself that you can do it.

Create affirmations that will help you move forward. Write these affirmations in your journal and use them regularly. Affirm, "I am making amends to those I have harmed," "I am a new person," "I accept responsibility for my past actions," "I am letting go of my guilt and shame."

Turn to your confidant for emotional support and reassurance and as a sounding board for your amends and reparations. Seek guidance before making any apology or reparation.

Choosing the Channel

Although there are many ways to make apologies, the number of channels through which direct apologies can be made is limited to four. Each option has its own advantages and disadvantages, which vary depending upon the circumstances. The four options are:

1. In person
2. By telephone
3. By letter
4. By e-mail

The advantages of each channel are relatively obvious, but it might be worth pointing out some of them. An in-person apology affords greater intimacy and a wider spectrum of communication possibilities (facial expression, tone of voice, body language, and an extra dimension that comes only with face-to-face communications). Face-to-face apologies permit a deeper exchange of emotion and facilitate greater understanding because they involve feedback, allowing the parties to react to one another, to clarify, and to modify their comments as necessary. A telephone call shares the exchange characteristics of face-to-face meetings, but it lacks the intimacy and the deeper dimension of understanding that physical presence provides. However, the telephone can be substituted when face-to-face meetings aren't feasible for one reason or another.

A letter, definitionally, affords only one-way communication. It is subject to misinterpretation, requires some skill in writing, and can't be modified in response to feedback. It is generally more difficult to convey complex thoughts and emotions in writing than in conversation. An e-mail has the same characteristics as a letter, except that it's not as personal, and the feedback, if it occurs, is likely to be faster. On the other hand, a letter or e-mail is preferable in certain situations and even mandated in others, such as with individuals who won't agree to see you or who won't take your telephone call.

A letter is preferable to personal contact when the recipients of your apology are dangerous, threatening, or irrational due to mental illness or out-of-control emotions. In such cases or where you are likely to encounter such serious resistance to your attempted apology that you will be verbally attacked, if not vilified, choose your channel carefully. Remember that the goal is to make an apology for what you have done wrong and to describe whatever reparations you intend to make, if any reparations can be made. That's all you have to do in this part of Step Five. You don't have to submit to abuse while you're doing it.

Making the Difficult Apology

In many instances, you will be delighted, even surprised, by the warm reception your apology receives. You may even be forgiven. Although you may expect, or at least hope, to have your apology gratefully received, you cannot know for sure what will happen. If your apology is well received and you obtain forgiveness for whatever you did wrong, your experience may end as a pleasurable one. But apologies do not always turn out that way. In some cases, you will be met with hostility, if you are received at all, and you will not be forgiven. You will be listened to coldly, lectured about your behavior, and told to leave.

When the lecture is deserved, listen to the charges and complaints. If the criticism is deserved, accept the validity of the other party's words and acknowledge them. Whatever pain you feel is part of the price you pay for your actions and for letting go of your regrets. If the words are not valid, however, ignore them. You have not come to defend yourself but to make an apology. In the final analysis, the response of the other parties to your apology does not matter. Yes, it would be nicer if they accepted your apology and forgave you, but their acceptance and forgiveness are not necessary for the success of the amend or for letting go of your regret. The only forgiveness that counts is your higher power's and the forgiveness you offer yourself (which will come with Step Nine). All that Step Five requires is to make the necessary amends. How those amends are received is irrelevant to the completion of the step and to letting go of your regrets.

The following guidelines will prove helpful when making difficult apologies to the parties to your regret:

- Prepare for the apology through prayer, creative visualization, journaling about your feelings, and discussions with your confidant.
- Approach the other parties as calmly, honestly, and openly as you can, focusing on your single goal: to make an apology and leave.
- In making your apology, do not grovel. You have not come to beg forgiveness but to offer an apology, describe the reparations you have in mind (if reparations are appropriate), and leave.
- Include all the components of an effective apology: acknowledgment of inappropriate behavior, acceptance of responsibility for that behavior and its negative consequences, expression of regret, request for a pardon, and assurance of nonrepetition and future behavioral change.
- Restrict your comments to what *you* have done wrong. Clean up your

side of the street without looking at his side of the street. Ignore his contributions to the regret, no matter how serious they were and even if they were the primary cause of the regret. Put aside the terrible things he has done to you. Acknowledge whatever responsibility you have in the regret, whatever mistakes you made, or whatever actions you took that created the regret, made the regret worse, or harmed the other party about which you feel guilty and for which you need to apologize.

- Refuse to get into an argument over your role in the regret or over his role in the regret. Do not become defensive, condemn him, lecture him, point out his faults, or otherwise blame him for any part in your regret. You have come to admit your mistakes, not to find his.
- Do not ask him to apologize or to make amends for his actions.
- If he becomes verbally or physically abusive, leave at once. He has a right to share his feelings about your behavior, but he does not have a right to call you names or to otherwise attack you verbally or physically.

Even if your apology is totally rejected, you will have accomplished what you set out to do. You will have completed this part of Step Five. And you will have traveled farther down the road to freedom.

Chris entered recovery from alcoholism and drug addiction when he was eighteen. His adolescence had been filled with anger, rebellion, problems at school, and minor run-ins with the law. After getting clean and sober at the end of the summer of his graduation from high school, he worked a year at construction to support himself while he tried to get his life together. At the end of that year, he decided to go to college and applied to a local community college, which accepted him. He worked at his construction job during the day, studied hard at night, and did well. About the same time, his regret over the pain and problems he had caused his parents while in high school grew into a burden that he could no longer tolerate.

Chris knew that he would have to make amends to his parents to let go of the guilt he felt and the regret he carried, but it would not be easy. For one thing, his parents were alcoholics themselves and were not in recovery. They blamed him for all the problems that he had created during his adolescent years and for many that he had not. While they were willing to see him, it had to be on their terms. It was clear that they had no apologies to make. Chris's amends were further complicated by his father's fits of rage, especially prevalent when he was drinking, that had led to beatings when Chris was younger and to threats of beatings when he was old enough to defend himself.

Chris made a list of all the ways in which he had harmed his parents and for which he wanted to apologize. The list was as complete as he could make it and included many different categories of harm, each with specific examples. Those categories varied from the worry he had caused them by repeatedly not coming home or telling them where he was to the legal fees they had incurred to get him out of trouble with the law.

In contemplating his apology, Chris worked closely with his confidant and used various spiritual and psychological tools to prepare himself for making it. He knew that his parents would accept no responsibility for their abandonment of his emotional needs or for the physical abuse they had administered over the years, but he was not there to ask for their apology. Chris's goal was to make his amends without getting angry or attacking them for all the ways in which they had hurt him.

When he was ready, Chris made an appointment to see his parents at their house. When he arrived, they were drinking, which made the encounter even more difficult. After he had refused a beer for the third time and had been lectured on not staying in touch with them and not helping with things around the house that needed to be done, Chris was finally permitted to speak. He explained that he had come to apologize for the behavior of his teenage years and for the fear and pain he had caused them. He said that most of what he had done was the result of his alcoholism and drug addiction but that he was not using that as an excuse. He was accepting full responsibility for his actions.

Chris went down his amends list, apologizing for categories of misdeeds, illustrated by specific examples, and assuring his parents that he would never behave that way again. He was often interrupted by his father, who expanded on the problems he had caused, sometimes getting angry at the memories, and by his mother, who cried intermittently. Chris refused to take the bait when they blamed him for things that he hadn't done, simply dismissing it in his mind and trying to listen patiently until he could move to the next item on his list.

As Chris went through the long list of amends, his father grew increasingly angry. He had continued to drink, and he started cursing and calling Chris names. At that point, Chris explained that he would not be subjected to abuse, that he was leaving, and that he would send the rest of his apology by letter. That challenge to his parental authority further enraged his father, and Chris left immediately and quickly under threat of physical attack.

Chris completed his apology the next day by writing a letter to his parents, explaining that he could not finish the apology in person because his father had physically threatened him, and he would no longer take that kind of abuse. Although Chris would have preferred an apology from his parents, some sympathy for his struggle with alcohol and drugs, and an expression of admiration that he had been clean and sober for eighteen months, he did not get them. From Chris's point of view, however, his apology was a success. It had not gone the way he had hoped it might, but it was not far from what he had expected it would be. With his apology over, Chris felt a great burden of guilt lifted from him. He had no reparations to make to his parents. With the change in his behavior that he had already engineered, his amends were now complete.

Reconciliations

When reconciliation with an estranged party is one of your goals, your amend will be somewhat different from the amends you make to those you don't like or even despise and never want to interact with again. The structure of the amend itself won't change. It will still require an apology, reparations, and changed behavior. The difference is in the apology: You will hold open the possibility of a reconciliation. You may offer to continue the conversation when the other party is ready, for example, or to develop ground rules for a renewal of the relationship. You can't insist on such a possibility, of course, but you can express a desire for it.

Reconciliation is not an essential part of an amend. From the standpoint of being relieved of guilt, completing Step Five, or letting go of regrets, no reconciliation is necessary. In some cases, a reconciliation isn't possible and perhaps would not be desirable. For example, you might not seek a reconciliation because of the nature of the harm done to you or because of the emotional state or distorted beliefs of the other party. It is possible to forgive and still not be reconciled, as you will discover in the forgiveness steps (Eight and Nine).

Amends to the Deceased or Unreachable: The Healing Letter

Some of the people to whom you owe amends may not be reachable. Perhaps they have died or have moved away and you cannot find them. In such cases, you will still need to make amends to them, because amends are made primarily for your benefit, not for the injured party's. It may satisfy those you have harmed to hear your apology, but that is not the reason you're making it. You can still apologize, make reparations, change your behavior, and get right with yourself and the world without getting in touch with the injured party.

When you cannot reach those you have harmed, you will have to be creative in developing analogous or metaphorical ways of making amends. One way to apologize to someone who is dead or missing is through a letter you write and actually mail, a letter that is never received. This type of letter is a psychological device for communicating with someone who is no longer living or is otherwise unreachable. Human beings are highly symbolic creatures. A letter that is written and mailed is a powerful psychological substitute for the real thing—even if it isn't received. When combined with prayer and visualizations, the healing letter is more effective still.

A healing letter can achieve many different objectives. It can, for example, express the love you felt but never articulated during a deceased person's lifetime. Consuela was raised in a family that expressed little verbal or physical affection. When her father died, she found herself desperately regretting that she had never told him how much she loved him. She also hadn't thanked him for the things he had made possible in her life, including a college education, which he had taken a second job to provide. The healing letter was Consuela's opportunity to say what she longed to say, to express the love she felt, and to convey her gratitude for the sacrifices her father had made and the gifts he had given her. Consuela sent the letter, without a return address, to the house she had grown up in, but with two of the numerals changed to a create a nonexistent street address. In Consuela's mind, the letter would find its way to her father but not to the house.

Consuela also visualized herself telling her father how much she loved him and how grateful she was for all he had given her over the years. In that visualization, Consuela watched her father smile in response to her words. She heard him express his own gratitude for her life and his own regret that he had not been more expressive of his love for her, which had never wavered.

Kurt also wrote a healing letter to his father, but it was to apologize for the pain he had caused and to seek forgiveness. In the letter, Kurt described his regrets, apologized for his actions, and listed the changes in his behavior and in his life that had resulted from those regrets. The healing letter was Kurt's opportunity to express his "if only's," the things he wished he had said and done that he did not say or do and all the things he did that he wished he hadn't done. The letter was also Kurt's chance to request forgiveness. He sent his letter to the address of the last house his father had lived in but to a city that had no such street. He included no return address. Kurt also used creative visualizations with his amends, finding peace and forgiveness in the imagined words of his dying father, whom he embraced.

Since no one but you will read the healing letter, write with honesty and deep emotion. Hold nothing back. The healing letter is like a creative visualization but on paper. It has the power to seem real and so to heal. Be specific and thorough. Write from the heart, knowing that the recipient, in some mysterious way, will receive and read your letter.

When your regrets are complicated or long-standing, more than one letter may be necessary. Perhaps many letters will be required for you to feel that your amends have been made. It doesn't matter how many letters it takes. You will know when you have written the last letter.

Amends to the Self

In the traditional view of the world, human beings have three relationships they must manage effectively in order to find real satisfaction and true happiness: the relationship they have with themselves, the relationship they have with other people, and the relationship they have with their higher power. The three relationships are interrelated, so that one bad relationship affects the other two relationships. If you do not like yourself, for example, it is difficult to like other people. If you are angry at your higher power, you are more likely to be angry with yourself or others.

All three relationships need to be nurtured for a life of fulfillment and meaning. In this step, you have taken action to improve one of those relationships: your relationships with others, at least with those you have harmed. You have made amends to them. Through that process, however, you are also making amends to your higher power and to yourself. The changed behavior that you pledge as part of your amend to others is also appropriate as the changed behavior you promise yourself.

A specific amend to yourself may also be necessary, especially if you have directly hurt yourself in some way. Years of drug addiction, alcoholism, rage attacks, failed jobs, or squandered talents are examples of regrets that weigh heavily on people in terms of the high cost to themselves (as well as to many others, of course). In such cases, an amend to yourself is warranted as a means of getting over the guilt you feel about what you have done. As with all amends, there are three components to the self-amend: an apology, reparations, and changed behavior.

A self-apology is straightforward. You apologize to yourself as you would to anyone else you had harmed, including in your apology all the necessary elements. You may wish to make that apology in a quiet place that has meaning for you, allowing enough time to contemplate the significance of what you are doing and to feel the emotional impact of your words. Once the apology has been made, you can choose to accept it or not. However, part of the amend you make to yourself is accepting your own apology. If you cannot accept your apology, which really means that you can't forgive yourself, don't be concerned. You will forgive yourself in Step Nine, and your apology will be accepted then.

Reparations made to yourself have the same purpose as those made to others: repair the damage of the past to the best of your ability, given your present circumstances. In most cases, that will mean taking some kind of action. For example, if your regret is not having completed college and being stuck in a low-paying job, the reparation you make is to go back to college and complete your education. If your regret is that you have been focused on career, money, and material things at the expense of any selfless form of service to others, your reparation may be to take on a project in which you can serve others (such as working in a soup kitchen, teaching a child to read, or anything else where your particular talents can be brought to bear).

3. Change the Harmful Behavior

The third component of an amend is new behavior. Once you have apologized and made reparations for your regrets, it is your responsibility to change the behavior that caused your regret in the first place. Reparations are not enough if you continue the same behavior that created the regret. Part of your amend to the injured party and to yourself is to alter your future behavior. Apologies are empty words and reparations are hollow actions unless you do.

In Collin's case, for example, which was discussed earlier, the nature of his apology and the reparations he should make for his adultery were not immediately clear. But his amended behavior was: no more extramarital affairs. Thereafter, Collin will have to remain faithful to his wife or else seek a divorce if the marriage isn't working. Other forms of amended behavior may also be appropriate for Collin, such as working harder at his marriage or being more attentive to his wife. In Tony's embezzlement case, his amended behavior is also clear: no more stealing.

Some behavior is not easy to change, however, at least without external assistance. You may find that you are highly resistant to change for any number of reasons, some of which may be a mystery even to you. If you are incapable of changing the problem behavior on your own, seeking outside help will be part of your amend. It's critical that you change the behavior that is creating regrets in your life. That change is part of the amend you make to those you have harmed, but it is also part of the amend you make to yourself. If you are given to rage attacks, take an anger management course or seek the help of a mental health professional. If you are an alcoholic, enter treatment or join Alcoholics Anonymous. Do whatever you have to do to change the behavior patterns that created your regrets and that expose you to future regrets. Otherwise, the amends you have made to others and to yourself will be incomplete.

After working Step Five, you should feel some relief from the burden of guilt you have borne with your regrets. The humble act of admitting your mistakes and trying to correct them as best you can is a liberating experience. Having made your amends—apologies, reparations, and changed behavior—you are free from the tyranny of guilt. When you cut the cord of guilt, you break a major chain that binds you to your regrets.

Although you have completed the activities of Step Five, your work on the step is not finished and never will be, because the changed behavior component of your amend is intended for a lifetime. You must continue to work at sustaining your new behavior and at improving it through daily practice and, if necessary, additional outside help. For the purposes of the steps, however, you are ready to move on to the next one. Enjoy the rewards of having completed this difficult step. They are real and very much deserved. Congratulations!

Take some time off and have fun.

With the hard work of Step Five and the new freedom it has brought, you can now examine your regrets from a different, and more favorable, perspective. Despite all the pain, fear, and guilt of your regrets, they have also brought you lessons and gifts. In Step Six, you will explore the hidden and not-so-hidden contributions to your life that came from the regrets you harbor.

9

STEP SIX: IDENTIFYING LESSONS AND GIFTS

IN STEP SIX, we examine our regrets from a different perspective, one that explores the good that came out of them rather than the bad. Having spent the first five steps looking at the pain of our regrets and the extent of our accountability in creating them, we now consider the possibility that our regrets have benefited us. But how? By teaching us lessons and offering us gifts of great value.

The idea that our regrets have taught us lessons may not be as foreign as the idea that our regrets have brought us gifts. "I learned my lesson, but it was too expensive, and I got no gifts," Rory complained. Jay took a different approach to arrive at the same conclusion: "It wasn't my fault, so I don't see what I could have learned. As far as gifts, forget it." We may not like the idea that our regrets have lessons and gifts to offer, but they inevitably do. We may have to search to find them, however, and we will need to do so with an open mind.

Every road taken, like every road not taken, is filled with potential regrets. But every regret is filled with potential lessons and gifts. It is always that way. The lessons of the road we took may be easier to see than the gifts, but they are no more important. Great gifts are offered through our regrets. They are difficult to see, however, if we are stuck in resentments, blaming, anger, or self-pity.

It will be easier to let go of our regrets if we are willing to accept the lessons and the gifts they offer us. If we perceive that our regrets have served a useful purpose by teaching us something that we needed to learn or by bringing us something that we needed to experience, they will be less regrettable. They will have redeeming value for us.

The distinction between a lesson and a gift isn't crucial for purposes of this step. In general, a lesson is something we have learned from past events that we can apply to similar events in the future. Rosa's sheltered upbringing led her to be overly trusting and overly dependent on those with whom she dealt, especially if they were nice to her and seemed supportive. This naïveté cost her dearly after a series of financial mistakes based on misplaced trust. For example, she gave her social security number to a telephone solicitor she didn't know, and he used the number to steal her identity. After the theft, it took several years to straighten out her credit.

Rosa also failed to read the terms of her car loan, taking her salesperson's word for the nature of its terms, only to discover later that the interest rate was higher than she had been promised. She also lost most of the proceeds from the sale of her home through an ill-fated investment she failed to check out. She met the person who misinvested her money at a party for prominent people and assumed that he must be honest. This series of mistakes devastated her finances and left her angry. But they were only part of a much larger regret: not being properly prepared to deal with "the real world," as she put it. Rosa's regrets taught her valuable lessons that would protect her in the future, leading her to take greater responsibility for her life, especially her financial life. At the same time, she had to learn to strike a balance between being unduly naive and unduly cynical.

The gifts that come from regrets are not so much specific lessons applicable to the future as they are whole new perspectives on life, greater wisdom, or a more meaningful set of goals. Gifts may also take the form of people who came into our lives because of our regret. Gifts often meet psychological or spiritual needs that we didn't know we had or that couldn't be met through "normal" events.

When Enrique's wife took the children, moved out of their house, and filed for divorce because of his drinking, he was furious. Shortly thereafter, he was fired from his job for the same reason, and he received a DUI, which had the potential of keeping him from working again in his profession. These series of regrets—suddenly part of the larger regret of alcoholism—took him into treatment and then to Alcoholics Anonymous. In AA, he found sobriety and discovered a new way of life that was richer and more satisfying than anything he had experienced before or had even thought possible. When he was reunited with his family, his outlook had changed dramatically, and he refocused his life on a different set of values that proved to be profoundly rewarding. The gift of Enrique's new life came out of his regrets.

Fujio was cutting the limb off a tree in his backyard. The branch he was sawing fell unexpectedly against his ladder, knocking him to the ground and seriously injuring his arm and shoulder. He was forced to undergo two surgeries and painful physical therapy. Fujio deeply regretted getting on that ladder, and it was easy for him to fall into "if only" thinking. Yet the gifts he received from the fall and the subsequent recovery were substantial. From that regret, Fujio discovered the depth of his courage, the love of his family and friends, and the fragile nature of life.

The lessons and gifts of our regrets are of great value because, when we recognize and accept them, they contribute to our spiritual growth and psychological development. Lessons and gifts inevitably arise as a consequence of our regrets, and their recognition is important because they give our regrets meaning. When recognized, they can change our lives for the better. The question is not whether the lessons and gifts are there but whether we will identify and use them. They must be there, because problems are always a source of potential lessons and gifts if we are receptive to seeing them. Nobody's life is without problems, no matter how well hidden those problems may be.

For whatever reason, this is a world of difficulties with which we must cope (just as it is also a world of joys that we are privileged to experience). Joys, too, are sources of lessons and gifts. But the gifts of love, for example, are easier to identify than the gifts of tragedy. Difficulties are really challenges to us and important opportunities for growth, development, and personal triumph. "Life is suffering," Buddha taught as the first of the Four Noble Truths. But he also taught that once suffering is accepted as part of life, it is transcended and is no longer suffering. Difficulties, once accepted and dealt with effectively, no longer feel like difficulties. In our acceptance, we have transcended them.

But such transcendence is not easy.

The spiritual traditions of two millennia provide effective means for dealing with the disappointments, fears, and tragedies that characterize life—as well as its joys, rewards, and pleasures. Spiritual wisdom offers an alternative to the suffering and pain of regret. Our journey of letting go of regret is a journey of transcendence as well as a journey of psychological growth that will take us beyond the sadness, anger, and shame of our past. We cannot change our regrets—what happened to us or to other people— but we can change how we respond to those regrets and what we do about them. We can change their effect on us. We can transcend our regrets and let them go.

The distinguished American psychiatrist M. Scott Peck wrote an insightful book on meeting life's difficulties called *The Road Less Traveled*. It was published in 1978, became a decade-long best-seller, and profoundly affected the lives of many people. In the book, Dr. Peck offered a different perspective on life's problems and challenges, describing them as essential to psychological growth, personal achievement, and individual satisfaction. An examination of our lives and activities will prove the wisdom of that perspective.

We take on certain difficulties in life quite willingly and even with great enthusiasm. The challenges they represent inspire us, teach us new skills, lead us into the company of others, and reward us in many ways. Whenever we begin a new project around the house, for example, accept a new assignment at work, or undertake learning a new skill, we have accepted a new challenge with all the difficulties it promises us. Yet we readily take them on for their rewards. Looked at from this perspective, what could hand us a greater set of difficulties (and rewards) than having children? As first-time parents, we face innumerable challenges, immense uncertainty, and terribly high stakes. But the challenge is so rewarding that we often take it on again with a second child!

Why we actively seek challenges of various kinds gives us a clue as to why it might be profitable to take on problems not of our choosing and even why we might be given them. Such problems are opportunities for us to grow, to learn, and to share this knowledge and experience with others. The challenges we happily pursue are a model for handling the less desirable challenges in our lives: strategically and with the goal of learning from them. Once we get past the question of "Why me?" we can move to the question of, "How do I approach this and what can I learn from it or get out of it?" Accepting that no life is without problems allows us to see ourselves not as victims but as pilgrims. The issue is not whether we will have problems and regrets, because we will. The issue is whether we will triumph over them by learning from them and letting them go.

Working the Step

Step Six is worked in four parts. Part one is a search for lessons. Part two is a search for gifts. Part three is an application of the lessons and gifts to help ourselves. Part four is an application of the lessons and gifts to benefit others. The Action List for Step Six is shown in the following chart:

Action List: Step Six

Identifying Lessons and Gifts

1. Identify the lessons of each regret
2. Identify the gifts of each regret
3. Apply the lessons and gifts for the benefit of ourselves
4. Apply the lessons and gifts for the benefit of others

Each item on the Action List is more fully described in the following paragraphs.

1. Identify the Lessons of Each Regret

To identify the lessons of our regrets, we have to consider both the lessons that we have actually learned and the lessons that we can still learn if we recognize and act on them. Most of us are aware of the lessons that our regrets have taught us. But we may be much less aware of the lessons that we might still learn from our regrets. This Action List item, therefore, consists of two parts: identifying the lessons of which we are aware and identifying the potential lessons of which we are still unaware.

Lessons I Have Learned

In journaling for this Action List item, describe the lessons you have learned from the events of each regret. The more lessons you can list, the greater the value your regret will have. This list of lessons should include small lessons as well as big ones. Many of these lessons will be obvious to you, but some may not be. For example, perhaps you made a commitment to enhance your work skills after you were laid off several years ago, but you had not thought of the new skills as a lesson of your regret, since they are so familiar to you now. In developing your list, seek the assistance of your confidant and others within your circle of friends. Your confidant can be especially effective in helping you mine your regrets for the lessons you have learned but have not recognized as coming from those regrets.

Confidants and friends can also help you test the validity of those lessons and prevent you from drawing the wrong lesson from the events of a regret. For example, an executive stole from his company and the embezzlement was discovered. He concluded that the lesson of his regret was that he should have been cleverer in designing his embezzlement scheme. That was the wrong lesson to draw.

Sadie's husband, who was an alcoholic, divorced her because, according to him, she had driven him to drink with her constant complaints about his drinking. Sadie concluded that the divorce was her fault and that her husband's drinking had been, too. Both conclusions were erroneous and so was the lesson she drew from the regret: she should have tried harder to get her husband sober and worked harder to save their marriage. But it wasn't within her power to get her husband sober, nor had the marriage failed because of her. Sadie drew the wrong lesson from her regret, and so it was no lesson at all.

Lessons to Be Learned

Now that you have described the lessons of your regret, you can use them as a basis from which to search for potential lessons. Potential lessons are the lessons the regret still holds for you—valuable lessons that can benefit you now and in the future but only if you recognize and act on them. They often have to be pieced together since they are not necessarily obvious. Like conclusions drawn from many factors or concepts built from different principles, potential lessons may take time to develop. In some cases, they cannot be seen until well after the events of the regret.

The following examples will get you started on creating a list of potential lessons from your regret:

- "I learned that seeking revenge was not a good idea. It did not turn out to be fulfilling, and it created even greater problems for me."
- "I learned not to be naive in business. It isn't a sign of distrust to have everything in writing. It just makes good business sense, because genuine misunderstandings do develop."
- "You need to make time for the people you love. Nothing else is more important. Every time you say no to being with them, you have lost that opportunity forever."
- "If you wait to do something until everything is just right for its success, you'll never do it. At some point, you have to move forward even if conditions aren't ideal."
- "I learned to follow my intuition."
- "I found out that you can't always be right, and you can't always win and that you may as well get used to it."
- "I discovered that if you can't learn to stand up for yourself, no one else will do it for you."
- "I realized that those you love can be taken without warning and that there is no such thing as forever. You have to enjoy them now, every minute, while you can."

Wisdom is often a lesson of our regrets. Much of what parents have to share with their children and what friends share with each other is gleaned from the harsh experience of regrets as well as from the sweet lessons of success. When regrets are studied to harvest their wisdom, they offer a rich learning field. But we have to be willing to do the spadework to find them.

2. Identify the Gifts of Each Regret

Your search for the gifts of your regrets will follow the same process you used in searching for lessons. Gifts are so closely allied with lessons that they are often indistinguishable. The difference between the two doesn't matter as long as the gift is recognized in one category or the other. Some gifts are direct, such as discovering how much someone loved you after she died. Others are indirect, as when a job termination leads to a new and more satisfying career.

Some of your gifts may have appeared almost simultaneously with the regret, while others may have come slowly over time. Some gifts are cumulative in nature and difficult to recognize because they are incremental. Your confidant and friends can help you recognize these gifts because of their greater objectivity and their long-term perspective on you and your regrets.

The following examples of gifts will help you get started on your list.

- "I discovered an inner strength I never knew I had."
- "I found out what it was like to be loved."
- "I grew up after the tragedy. I needed to grow up, to accept responsibility, so that part of it, anyway, turned out to be a good thing."
- "I discovered that I was courageous. I had never known that before."
- "I learned to love as a result of it, really to love."
- "It forced me into recovery from my drug addiction."
- "I renewed my faith, and I found a richer, deeper relationship with God."
- "I discovered that I had something to offer other people."
- "It changed me. I became a better person. I'm more willing to listen. I'm more compassionate, less quick to judge."
- "I never took another day or another person for granted after that."

- "I knew I had to give up my rage. It was destroying me and the people I loved. I went into therapy."
- "It redirected me toward service to others and away from a preoccupation with myself."
- "I developed a passion for life that I had never had before."

Benefits that compensate to some degree for the inevitable losses of life constitute a special category of gifts worth identifying. In one sense, all the gifts of our regrets compensate us in some way. The compensation may not be sufficient in our view to make up for the losses of the regret, but it is compensation nonetheless, and its recognition makes it easier to let go of that regret. What makes the compensating gifts of inevitable losses particularly interesting is that they are built into the source of the regret. Juan and Lucinda, for example, suffered an inevitable loss when their twin girls left for college. It was a painful experience for the two parents but necessary if their daughters were to reap the benefits of a college education. Those benefits were a compensating gift. Other gifts included having more time for other interests (Lucinda went back to work, for example), more time to spend together in the evenings, and an atmosphere around the house that was a bit more serene. The girls' growing maturity was also a welcome change. Having their children leave home was an inevitable loss of the passage of time. Had the parents bemoaned the loss of their children without searching for the compensating gifts, the pain of the inevitable loss they regretted would have been much greater.

In the same way, people leaving middle age may not like the loss of youthful energy, but the potential compensating gifts include greater wisdom and competence. These gifts can be welcomed and savored, or they can be ignored and rejected by focusing on what was lost rather than on what was gained. Toward the end of life, of course, inevitable losses grow more severe, and the gifts grow more spiritual and sometimes more difficult to accept and understand. Even so, regretting, as opposed to accepting, is unproductive. It is easier to accept the things we like than to accept the things we don't like, but acceptance is fundamentally a spiritual and psychological process that allows us to transcend events in our environment. Acceptance is a state we create within ourselves that allows us to make peace with external factors, regardless of whether we like them.

A special Action List has been included to help you structure your search for gifts. For each regret, describe all the gifts that come to mind in each of the eight categories, but don't worry about distinctions among the categories. Compensating gifts may fit into more than one category.

Action List: Step Six

Gifts of the Road I Took

1. People
2. Interests
3. Opportunities
4. Successes
5. Psychological gifts
6. Spiritual gifts
7. Other gifts
8. Potential gifts

Complete this Action List for each regret in accordance with the following guidelines:

1. *People:*   Describe the loves of your life that came out of your regret, whether romantic loves, good friendships, or deepened existing friendships. These are the people you met or who became more important to you as a result of your regret. They may have inspired you, counseled you, or supported you at critical times or on a continuing basis. In each case, they offered you the priceless gifts of being loved and having someone to love. Who are these people, and what individual gifts did they bring you?

2. *Interests:*   What interests or passions did you develop because of your regret? After Sandra's only child died of a rare blood disorder, she devoted her time to raising public awareness of the disease, increasing

funds for medical research, and finding a cure. In the process, she helped many people and found emotional support from other parents like herself who had lost a child to the disease.

3. *Opportunities:* What opportunities came your way because of the regret, including jobs and opportunities for service to others? For example, a sentence of community service might have opened your eyes to the joys of volunteering or working with those less fortunate than yourself.

4. *Successes:* What successes have you had, large or small, that resulted from something the regret forced you to do? When Edwin was in elementary school, a deranged man threatened to detonate a bomb on the playground where he and other children were playing at recess. His teacher calmly talked with the man, trying to draw him away from the school building, while telling the children to return to their classrooms. The man grew impatient and triggered the bomb. The explosion killed the teacher and two students who had lagged behind. Edwin escaped death, but the force of the blast tore off part of his leg, forcing its amputation above the knee. When Edwin entered junior high school wearing his prosthetic leg, he developed an interest in the mechanics of artificial limbs and how legs and knees could be made to fit better and to work better. That interest in artificial limbs followed him into college and grad school and then into a highly successful career, where he developed innovative artificial knee designs that helped thousands of amputees.

5. *Psychological gifts:* In having to deal with the consequences of your regret, how did you grow psychologically? What victories over yourself or over adversities came out of the regret? How did those victories change you and give you something to share with others who found themselves in similar situations? List the positive attributes such as self-confidence, self-discipline, or acceptance of responsibility that you acquired or strengthened as a result of your regret.

6. *Spiritual gifts:* What spiritual gifts did your regret bring or enable you to develop as a result of its consequences? For example, perhaps you developed greater tolerance and compassion for others or a deeper faith. Perhaps the regret taught you that material success

devoid of loving relationships or a commitment to principled behavior was meaningless. Perhaps the regret led you to greater trust in others, to a desire to be of greater service, or to a recognition of your need for a power greater than yourself. Perhaps you learned how to love or to accept the love of others.

7. *Other gifts:*   You may have received gifts that do not fit neatly into any of the other categories. If so, write about them here.

8. *Potential gifts:*   Ask yourself what gifts are potentially yours to receive that you have not yet recognized or have not taken advantage of in some way. Talk with your confidant and your friends to help you with this search. The more gifts you find, the more meaningful your regret will be, and the easier it will be to accept that the regret had value for you and served a purpose. Even if you have found several gifts, ask yourself what additional gifts await your discovery. Consider, for example, how the events and consequences of your regrets could still make you stronger, more honest, or more grateful. How could your regrets teach you humility, patience, or persistence? How could they make you more loving or more committed to living life fully and richly? How could you use them to find or deepen your faith in a higher power?

Return to the list of categories that you used to describe the gifts of your regrets. This time, search for *potential* gifts—gifts that could still be yours if you were to recognize them or work to get them. The question you are seeking to answer is, "How can I make my regrets even more valuable for me?"

3. Apply the Lessons and Gifts for the Benefit of Ourselves

Once you have identified the lessons and gifts of your regrets, you are in a position to use them for your benefit. When you apply them to help yourself (or others), your regrets will lose some of their sting. While it's true that your regrets have deprived you of something valuable, they have also brought you something of value. You may not see the exchange as equal, and it may not be. The death of a child is too high a price to pay for whatever lesson or gift might result. But there are still powerful lessons and gifts inherent in the most devastating regrets. Acknowledging these lessons and gifts and using them to improve your life is an important part of letting go of your regrets.

Consider the following examples as you ponder some of the ways in which you can apply the lessons and gifts of your regrets:

- A profound regret over having missed the big events of his oldest son's life led Pepe to reject a promotion to a still more demanding job. Instead, he took less pay in a position that required little travel so that he could spend more time with his two younger children. Pepe's regret caused him to reprioritize his time, reevaluate the importance of his career, and change the goals he had set for himself.
- Bankruptcy from credit card debt taught Ling and her husband fiscal restraint, the value of a budget, and the necessity of saving. They learned to spend less and so to live within their means, paving the way for a more secure financial future.
- Jake's heart attack forced him to determine what was most important in his life. "It was," he said, "the best thing that ever happened to me. It changed my whole perspective, and I acted on it, changing my lifestyle and my priorities."

Regrets can teach us:

- To follow our intuition.
- To relish every moment we spend with the people we love.
- To realize the limitation that material things have to make us happy or to bring about a deep and lasting satisfaction.
- To say "I love you" to those we do love.
- To make amends when we need to make them.
- To become more self-disciplined.
- To tell the truth.

Examine the lessons and gifts that you have identified for each of your regrets, and describe in your journal:

- How you have used them to benefit yourself.
- New ways in which you might use them to benefit yourself.

4. Apply the Lessons and Gifts for the Benefit of Others

The lessons and gifts of your regrets can be used to help others as well as yourself. When you take advantage of that opportunity, you profit again from your regrets and make their consequences more bearable. Rather than a set of experiences that brought you only pain, your regrets become a source of wisdom, which you can share with others. Asked why he thought there was so much suffering in the world, a man once replied, "Without it, we would have no need of one another. You would have no reason to help other people, and they would have no opportunity to help you."

You can use the lessons of your regrets to help others who can profit from what you have learned and from what you have to share. You can support other people emotionally and spiritually and help them find hope, courage, and answers when you have suffered as they have. Your lessons can be an example, your gifts an inspiration, and your letting go a model. Whatever your lessons and whatever your gifts, there is someone with whom you can share them. There is someone for whom your regrets can make a difference.

In helping others, of course, you also help yourself. Nothing takes a person out of self-pity, remorse, and regret as quickly as helping another human being. There is someone out there who needs you, someone who will appreciate you, and someone who will profit from what you know. There is also someone to remind you of how grateful you can be for what you have been given. By serving others, your own advantages in life become clearer and your own blessings more obvious.

To complete Step Six, describe for each of your regrets:

- How you have used its lessons and gifts to benefit others.
- New ways in which you could use its lessons and gifts to benefit others.

Applying the Spiritual and Psychological Tools

If you have trouble identifying the lessons and gifts of your regret or the ways in which they can be applied to benefit you and others, use the spiritual and psychological tools to gain the insights you need. For example, pray for the willingness to be open to the lessons and gifts of your regrets. Ask your higher power for the help you need to identify them and for the creativity to apply them imaginatively to benefit yourself and others. Pray for the courage to accept the good that has come from your regrets.

Visualize working the step. See yourself finding the lessons and gifts of your regrets, writing them in your journal, and marveling at what you have learned. Imagine applying them enthusiastically to help yourself and others in specific ways, finding satisfaction in these gifts that are now yours to give as a result of your regrets. See yourself being congratulated by your confidant for the rich harvest, and experience the joy you feel at having learned and been given so much.

Use thought analysis to think logically and creatively about ways to use the lessons and gifts of your regrets. Seek the counsel of your confidant and friends in your search to identify them and to apply them to benefit yourself and others. Affirm, "I am using the lessons and gifts of my regrets," "I am grateful for the lessons and gifts I have been given," and "I see the good that has come from my regrets."

As a result of working Step Six, you have found a redeeming feature to your regrets: lessons and gifts. Although you may not consider them worth the price you paid for them, they can be enormously valuable nonetheless. Your regrets, therefore, have not been a total loss. This more balanced view of your regrets is also a more realistic view, and it prepares you for Step Seven: developing compassion.

10

STEP SEVEN: DEVELOPING COMPASSION

IN STEP SEVEN, you will revisit your role in creating the regrets you harbor. This time, however, you will do so from the perspective of the past, not from the perspective of the present. With twenty-twenty hindsight, it is easy to see the mistakes you made that created your regrets. That does not mean, however, that you could have altered those actions or decisions at the time, given the circumstances that existed. It may be that you did the best you could have done.

The purpose of this step is to help you develop compassion for the way in which you have handled your regrets, including their creation. For that reason, the step may seem less relevant to regrets that happened *to* you, regrets that you were forced to deal with that were not of your own making. On the other hand, you have played some role in all the regrets that you continue to harbor. From the moment of their creation forward, your regrets were in your charge. What you did with them and how much you let them hurt you were entirely up to you. Therefore, the need for compassion exists with every regret you still hold, regardless of its cause.

Working the Step

When you cast judgment on yourself for the mistakes that led to your regrets, you do so from the perspective of the present. Yet the contexts of the present and the past are very different. *You* are probably very different compared to the way you were when your regret was created. In Step Seven, you will seek to answer this question: *Could I have handled my regrets any differently from the way I did at the time of their creation, given who I was and the circumstances that existed then?* However ineffective, inappropriate, or damaging your behavior may have been, was it nonetheless the best you could have done?

This line of thinking is tricky and even risky. Had you not prepared for it by working the first six steps, you might have pursued it with the goal of justifying your actions and avoiding accountability. But since you have completed those steps, you can hold yourself fully accountable for your actions in creating and maintaining your regrets, while you work to accept that you could not have acted any differently at the time, given the circumstance that existed then. In truth, regardless of what you did, nothing else was possible for you. What you did was the best you could have done, as flawed as it may have been. Or you would have done it differently. This realization does not make you any less accountable for your actions, but it should make you more compassionate in understanding the actions you did or didn't take.

Why does it help to think about your regrets in this way? Isn't this a trick to let yourself off the hook? Not if you still hold yourself accountable for what you did. In earlier steps, you accepted responsibility for your actions and made amends and reparations. In this step, you will not deny or minimize anything you have done or the negative consequences your behavior caused. What you will do is to accept that what you did was the only thing you could have done at the time.

Very likely, the actions you took that you now regret do not represent your essential self. They may have been actions you took while drunk or drugged that you would not have taken otherwise, things you didn't do because you were psychologically impaired, or acts you committed in severe emotional pain. As regrettable as your behavior may have been, it was the best you could manage then. That's what you're trying to accept. You could not have performed better and still have been the person you were. A recognition of this truth will allow you to develop some appreciation of your struggles, problems, and imperfections and how they led to the acts you later regretted. Like other human beings, you fell short of your ideals, the ideals of others, and, perhaps, even short of acceptable behavior. But it was all you could do.

When Joan betrayed her best friend to get ahead in her career, she rationalized it to herself as perfectly justifiable. A researcher for a small drug company, she stole her friend's idea and developed a patent that brought her fame and a fortune in royalties. Even as she spent the money and enjoyed the respect of her colleagues, she felt increasingly guilty—and empty. Her drive to succeed and the consuming demands of her career isolated her and kept her from meaningful relationships. As she grew progressively more lonely and unhappy, she remembered longingly the friends she used to have, the good times she once had shared with them, and the happiness she had felt in their presence. First among these friends was the one she had betrayed. She longed to rebuild the relationship but had no way of doing so. Her friend was dead.

As Joan struggled to make sense of what she had done, she thought back to the way she had been at the time of her betrayal and the beginning of her regret. She was not trying to excuse the betrayal or to minimize it, but she was trying to understand how she could have committed what she now considered a despicable act. She remembered how insecure she had been growing up in a poor family and how desperate she was to make money, to become famous, to do anything that would fill the emptiness inside her. She recalled how often her father had told her that she was foolish to get a graduate degree and that she would never make it the man's world of medical science. She remembered how driven she had been to prove him wrong, to impress him with her money and her success, and to gain his approval. She also recalled how selfish she had been in those days, how singularly concerned she was with herself, and how little she had counted friendships except as contacts to further her career.

By remembering these things, Joan began to develop compassion for herself. By going back to the way she was at the time of her regret and to the circumstances that existed then, she could begin to understand why she had done what she had. That understanding was no excuse and didn't make it any less wrong, but it helped Joan appreciate how it was that she gave in to a terrible temptation. She was no victim. She always had the power to make the choice that was morally right, but she did feel sadness for the empty, desperate woman she had been in her youth. Somehow, that sadness and her appreciation of how difficult her life had been helped her understand the poor choices she had made. She felt less like a monster than a very flawed young woman who made a horrendous mistake and then compounded it over the years. To have done better than she did, Joan decided, wasn't possible for her at the time. As tragic as that was, it was also true. She had been too impaired to do right. And she had suffered deeply for it ever since.

You may have trouble accepting such a compassionate approach toward your own regrets, because it sounds too easy, too much like an excuse for bad behavior, or too forgiving. Perhaps it would be if you had not patiently worked the first six steps. But you have proven, through those steps, that you are willing to accept responsibility for your actions and to make amends for them. You have stepped up to the plate and held yourself accountable. *Because you have done so,* you are now entitled to a broader, more inclusive perspective, one that encompasses your own limitations that existed at the time of your regret.

Like Joan, had you been able to do better, you would have. That you didn't indicates an impairment you could not overcome, a momentary stress that got the better of you, a challenge with which you were not prepared to deal. In other words, in your weakness, you were human—and paid the price of being human. By acknowledging and accepting with compassion and understanding who you *were then,* you can deal more effectively with who you *are now.* As a result of your amends, you have changed your behavior. You are not the same person you were when the regret was created.

Step Seven is not about forgiveness. It is about trying to develop compassion for yourself as a flawed human being, like all human beings, who struggled with challenges and opportunities and did not do as well as you wish you had. You have only to develop some empathy, some sympathy for the person you were then, even if "then" was only last month.

In this step, you will reevaluate your performance at the time of your regret. You will acknowledge your weaknesses, but you will also accept that you were not able to overcome them, given the emotional and other resources available to you at the time. In the process of looking at your regrets in this light, you will try to stop blaming yourself. Instead, you will seek acceptance of who you were then and how you tried to do the best you could, given what you had to work with at the time. As you let go of the blame and find acceptance, you will let go of your regrets and find compassion.

The compassion that you develop toward yourself in this step will prepare you to forgive others in Step Eight and to forgive yourself in Step Nine. As you accept that you did the best you could under the circumstances and grow more compassionate toward yourself, another possibility will dawn on you. Perhaps the people who hurt you could not have done better, either. Perhaps they were just like you: struggling with a set of problems and experiences that precluded them from acting in supportive or even acceptable ways. Perhaps they were in the same boat. Perhaps we all are. There may be some relief in that realization and some freedom. It does not mean that you hold anyone who hurt you any less accountable, but it does mean that you can develop compassion for them as well as for yourself.

There are three items on the Action List for Step Seven:

Action List: Step Seven

Developing Compassion

1. Assess your capacities at the time of the regret
2. Identify what you did right
3. Apply the spiritual and psychological tools

In working the step, apply all three Action List items to each regret.

I. Assess Your Capacities at the Time of the Regret

In addressing this Action List item, try to remember the way you were when your regret was created and the specific circumstances that existed at that time. Describe those circumstances in your journal. Include any emotional or physical problems you were dealing with that made it difficult for you to act in the way you would now have preferred. Describe the fear, shame, guilt, anger, financial hardship, or other factors that influenced the decisions you made. Ask yourself whether you could have done any better than you did, given the events of the time and where you were psychologically and spiritually. The question is not "should" you have done better but *could* you have done better. Realistically, what could you have done differently? If you are fair in your assessment, you will find that it would have been very difficult, if not impossible, for you to have behaved any way other than the way you did.

If the acts creating your regret were accidental, compassion for yourself may be easier to find since your actions were not intentional. Perhaps you could have been more careful, but in reality, accidents do happen—sometimes serious ones. If the cause of your regrets was unintentional, but you still blame yourself, work on figuring out why. Is there a toxic thought pattern involved, for example? If it's a question of forgiveness, you will deal with that issue in Steps Eight and Nine. Use the spiritual and psychological tools on this aspect of the step.

2. Identify What You Did Right

When regretting, many people fail to give themselves credit for what they did right, especially for the actions that lessened the consequences of their regrets. In some of your regrets, if not all of them, you may have acted to lessen their effects by preventing them from getting worse or by trying to correct the negative consequences as they were unfolding. As bad as it was, you could have made it much worse—but you didn't. By overlooking what you did right, you deny the efforts you made that were positive and so make it more difficult to be compassionate toward yourself. In examining your regrets for the purpose of identifying what you did right, it is not false praise that you're seeking. It's a realistic appraisal that gives you credit where credit is due.

Ken was an absent father whose job and intense desire to succeed at that job kept him from much interaction with his children, particularly his two sons, for whom he had little time. One of his greatest regrets, looking back, was his failure to be part of their lives and the distance he felt in their present relationship. The two boys respected him, but he didn't feel that he had ever bonded with them, and they were less likely than their sisters, as young adults, to want to spend the time with him that he wanted to spend with them. As he sought to come to terms with this regret, he tried to identify what he had done right with these two children.

The reason he had always used for his absences was the high standard of living he had provided for them. He could admit now that it was an excuse. In truth, he had been more interested in his job, success in his field, and the huge bonuses he had received than he was in relating to his children. He regretted that now and realized that the money was no substitute for having been part of their lives. Nonetheless, it did have positive effects, such as fine private-school educations, elaborate family vacations to interesting places, and many material things they seem to have enjoyed. Ken included these advantages in trying to identify some of the things he had done right in dealing with his sons. He had tried to see the boys as much as he could. That wasn't much, but he had made some sacrifices at work to be with them every once in a while. He had tried to teach them honesty, and he had never intentionally hurt them. To the best of his ability at the time, he had loved them. Those were some of the items Ken included on the list of what he had done right in the deep regrets he had about his sons.

In your journal, for each of your regrets, list:

- The ways in which you tried to lessen the negative consequences of your regret.
- The ways in which you didn't make the regret worse.

3. Apply the Spiritual and Psychological Tools

If you have trouble developing compassion for yourself and for your behavior in relation to your regrets, consider how you can use prayer, creative visualization, affirmations, sharing with others, and additional journaling to help you with this step. For example, in your prayers, ask that you be given compassion for yourself. Pray that you might remember your past without the prejudice of the present. Pray for a greater understanding of the context of your actions, why you did what you did, and why your behavior could not have been different, given who you were at the time of your regret. Ask your higher power to help you assess the state of your life as it was then, realistically and honestly.

Use creative visualization to remember yourself as you were when the regret was created, perhaps in emotional distress, perhaps impaired in some other way. See yourself as you are now reaching a hand out to yourself as you were then. See yourself taking that hand and then embracing yourself. Feel the condemnation leaving as you hug yourself, recognizing the sadness and pain of the life you were leading. Give into your feelings of sympathy and compassion for the person you were. Feel the joy of reconnecting with yourself, of letting go of the anger and the blame, replacing it with an appreciation of your struggles, a loving acceptance of who you were, and gratitude for who you are now becoming.

Journal about your difficulties in finding compassion for yourself, about your refusal to see any extenuating circumstances for your past behavior. Write about your fears of facing the person you were, the self-blame that's so hard to give up, your hopes for this step, and how freeing it would be if you could accept that you had done the best you could do.

Affirm, "I am compassionate toward myself," "I did the best I could at the time of my regret," "I am sympathetic and loving toward myself," and "I am proud of what I am becoming."

Use your confidant to explore your past, to help you see that you did the best you could under the circumstances, and that you are deserving of compassion.

On some days, you may feel more compassionate toward yourself than on others. But you should strive, over time, to build a strong and generous compassion for yourself, one that recognizes, appreciates, and even honors the difficulties, struggles, and defects of character that led you to the actions you now regret. In being compassionate, what you are attempting to do is to understand your inappropriate behavior in the context of your life and circumstances at the time of your regrets.

You are not *now* who you were *then*. The past belongs to the past. What happened cannot be changed, but *you* can be changed. You *have* changed. You are changing even now through these steps of letting go. It is time to look back on the past as an earlier period in your life in which you struggled with problems that were sometimes beyond your ability to manage well. It's time to close that chapter of your life and move on.

You did the best you could. You could have done worse. You didn't. For that, you can be grateful, giving yourself some credit for what you did right and what you did well in a difficult period of your life.

Take a deep breath. Breathe in compassion and sympathy for who you were. Breathe out blame and condemnation. Take another deep breath. Breathe in acceptance and gratitude. Breathe out resentments and disapproval. Take a third deep breath. Breathe in love for who you are now. Breathe out anger at who you were not then.

Now, if it is possible, go for a walk outside. Observe the flowers and the trees. Notice how each tree is different, even trees of the same species. Notice how each has been shaped by different forces, how some have been scarred, some are bent, and some have holes in their canopies from lost limbs. Observe how each tree, despite its defects, provides shade and adds beauty to the street. Then see how perfect each tree is, in its own way, even in its imperfections. You are like the trees, shaped by many different forces, scarred in some ways, but still beautiful to behold, even in your imperfections.

With the greater compassion developed from working Step Seven, you will turn your attention to Step Eight and the process of forgiving those who have hurt you in the regrets of your life. Step Eight is the door to freedom from regret. In Step Nine, you will forgive yourself and walk through that door.

11

Step Eight: Forgiving Others

WITH THE COMPLETION OF STEP SEVEN, you have reached the door to freedom from regret. You have only to open it and walk through.

The door to freedom has a brass plaque engraved with a single word: "Forgiveness."

In Step Eight, you will open the door by forgiving those who have hurt you.

In Step Nine, you will walk through it to freedom by forgiving yourself.

Forgiving those who have harmed you is the objective of this step. It is mandatory if you want to let go of your regrets. Nonforgiveness is the last chain that binds you to your regrets, to the past, and to the pain.

The Meaning of Forgiveness

Forgiveness is an often misunderstood word. Enduring myths about forgiveness have distorted its meaning in many people's minds, creating stumbling blocks that keep them in their unforgiveness. Forgiving is the process through which we come to terms with our regrets intellectually, emotionally, and spiritually so that they no longer have power over us. In forgiving, we let go of our resentments and our blame, our guilt and our shame, our anger and our sadness. We neutralize the power of what has happened in the past so that it no longer interferes with the present.

Forgiveness is not an event or a by-product of something else but a deliberate choice. It is not a casual act or an offhand statement made without forethought but the result of an intellectual and spiritual decision that we support with our feelings.

Forgiveness is not something that we can be coerced into giving. It must be given freely, or it is not forgiveness at all. It is an act of generosity that, like all such acts, is a greater gift to us than to the recipient. *It is not for others that we forgive. It is for ourselves.* We are our primary concern in forgiving, although it is commonly thought to be the other party. The forgiveness we grant to others may have little or no effect on them, but it doesn't matter. It will have a powerful effect on us.

Forgiveness is a paradox that, like other paradoxes, does not seem to make sense. Why should forgiving others help us when it is the other person who is being forgiven? Why should we forgive when there is no apology or amend from the offending party? How can we forgive acts that are "unforgivable"? The answer to these and similar questions is the same: We do it because it is what we must do to be free ourselves—free of the anger, the pain, the person, or the events that have harmed us. We do it to free ourselves from their power to hurt us still. That is the primary reason we forgive.

Forgiveness is a skill that improves with practice. It is also a commitment. In many instances of deep regrets, we may not be able to forgive completely the first time we try. We may have to forgive over and over, with each effort producing a longer period of forgiveness until the periods run together into permanence. Each time will be easier, however, as we master the art of forgiving.

The Benefits of Forgiving

The benefits of forgiving far outweigh the imagined benefits of withholding forgiveness. There is no comparison between the two. Forgiving is a bold and enterprising act. It is neither passive nor weak but an expression of courage and power. Only the strong and the brave can truly forgive. Forgiving is one of the most freeing of all human actions, because it is grounded in love. It releases us from the domination of unhappy memories, disturbing events, hostile people, and bitter regrets. The benefits of forgiving are rich and real. They include the following:

Forgiving Brings Health Benefits

In addition to the substantial psychological and spiritual benefits of forgiving, medical research indicates that forgiveness conveys physical health benefits as well. It lowers heart rates and blood pressure and gives people a greater sense of control over their lives. It reduces anger, stress, and depression, and it increases vitality and optimism. In contrast, withholding forgiveness leads to higher stress levels and greater feelings of sadness and anger. The bitterness, rage, fear, and resentments that come from withholding forgiveness raise the level of cortisol, a fight-or-flight hormone. Over time, elevated cortisol levels can lead to heart attacks, strokes, coronary disease, ulcers, colitis, and immune system problems.

Forgiving Frees Us from the Captivity of the Offender

When we refuse to forgive, we turn control of our emotional life over to the very people who hurt us in the first place. Once again, they victimize us but this time with our permission. We are no longer just the victim; we have become our own tormentor. By forgiving, we sever our emotional and psychological ties to the offending events or parties. They lose their power to hurt us or to affect our behavior or emotional life in any way. They no longer absorb our energy or our thoughts, which we can devote to happier and more productive purposes.

Forgiving Allows Us to Pursue Practical Approaches to Resolving Difficulties Involving the Offender

Forgiving allows us to take the most practical and productive approach to resolving issues that still involve the offending party. José, for example, was involved in a prolonged and bitter divorce, with court fights over custody and alimony dragging out for months and months. The angrier he became at his former wife's behavior, the more desperate he grew to hurt her. Then he devised an ingenious plan to get back at his ex-wife, which, unfortunately, required him to use his children against her. José's slow realization that he was willing to hurt his children to get to their mother shocked him into rethinking his approach to coping with the divorce.

José finally decided he needed to cool down and come to terms with his own actions. In the process, he tried to forgive his ex-wife and let go of the regrets associated with their divorce. When he was finally able to forgive her, he was freed of his resentments and his desire to hurt her. José could then act in the best interests of his children and himself, regardless of the positive effect of his actions on his former spouse. He was free.

We Get On with Our Lives

When we free the energy trapped in the anger and hatred of our regrets, we can use it for productive purposes that further our personal relationships, our career, and our lives. While we are stalled in our regrets, consumed by resentments and thoughts of revenge, the people who hurt us may well be moving on. By forgiving them, we regain the energy and focus we need to concentrate again on making our lives rewarding and fruitful. A rich, meaningful life is, after all, the best "revenge."

When Natalia's long-term boyfriend found out she was pregnant, he agreed to marry her but only on the condition that she abort the child. Tormented by the impossible demand of having to choose between her boyfriend and her baby, Natalia reluctantly agreed to the abortion. After it was over, her boyfriend left her. Devastated by the loss of the child and the betrayal of the man she loved, Natalia fell into a depression, then into blaming, and then into rage. Only after she forgave her boyfriend, which she had to do in order to let go of the regret, could she also let go of the anger and the rage. When she did, she was able to seek a new romantic relationship, recapture the joie de vivre she had lost after the breakup, and carry out her work with the same degree of competence she had once exhibited. She was able to move on with her life.

Myths of Forgiveness: What Forgiving Others Is Not

To understand what forgiveness is and how the process of forgiveness works, it helps to understand what forgiveness is not. Persistent myths distort our understanding of what forgiveness is and what it entails. These myths block many people from forgiving. Some of the most common myths are described in the following paragraphs.

To Forgive, We Have to Forget the Offending Behavior

"I will never forget what he did to me. I will never forget the beatings," Martina says, and she is right. She will remember them for a lifetime. But that does not mean that she cannot forgive her former husband. Forgetting is not part of forgiving. With forgiveness, we let go of the past in order to reclaim the present, but we do not forget that past. The memories remain, but their power to hurt us does not. It is gone.

To Forgive Is to Excuse the Offending Behavior

Forgiveness does not in any way excuse or condone the inappropriate actions that created our regret. If Matt were to discuss his father's incestuous behavior toward him as a boy, he would continue to use the same adjectives that rightfully condemn it for the awful series of acts that it was. He does not say that his father's actions were acceptable then or excusable now. In fact, he still abhors them. Yet he forgave his father. He forgave him for only one reason: to be free of him. Through forgiveness Matt could let go of the hatred of his father, accept that his father had had some good qualities, and make peace with that part of his life, as horrible as it had been.

When We Forgive, We No Longer Hold the Person Accountable for the Offending Behavior

Accountability remains after we grant forgiveness to a perpetrator. Accountability never ends. We can forgive people and still believe they should be held responsible for their actions, including being sentenced to prison. We can forgive and still ask for a divorce or sue for damages. Forgiveness never implies that accountability has been waived. When their teenage daughter was raped and killed, Ralph and Edith forgave her killer. They did that for their sakes, not his. They still agreed with the jury that the young killer should spend the rest of his life in prison without the possibility of parole. Their forgiveness was real, but so was their satisfaction that he had been held accountable for his crime.

When We Forgive, We Are Implying That the Offender Is Innocent, Less Guilty, or Somehow off the Hook

Forgiveness does not imply a lack of guilt. In fact, the opposite is true. There is no need to forgive the innocent. Only the guilty need our forgiveness. But we grant that forgiveness for ourselves, not for them. Gretl forgave her brother for looting the family business and driving it into bankruptcy, which wiped out most of her assets. She forgave him *not* because he was innocent but because he wasn't. Her forgiving action did not make him less guilty; it acknowledged and confirmed his guilt. But it freed her from debilitating anger and hatred and allowed her to refocus on rebuilding her assets and enjoying her life.

We are not letting people off the hook when we forgive them, although they may think we are. It is true that in some cases, our forgiveness may lessen another person's suffering and regret to some degree, *but only if he or she cares.* Many people against whom we hold resentments care little or nothing about what we think of them, much less whether we forgive them. In fact, our torment may actually please them. As a result, the offending party may not be suffering at all because of our lack of forgiveness. The only certainty is that *we* are suffering from our refusal to forgive. Whether the other parties care enough about us to suffer from a lack of forgiveness cannot be known to us. But it doesn't matter, because the degree of their suffering cannot possibly compare to ours when we refuse to forgive. Withholding forgiveness is like taking poison and expecting the other person to die.

To Forgive, We Have to Reconcile with the Offender

To reconcile with someone is to reestablish a relationship with that person. Reconciliation does not have to be part of forgiving. It can be, but only if we choose to make it so. When Sam went off to Vietnam, his wife moved another man into their house. She lived with him for the two years Sam was in Southeast Asia. When Sam returned from active duty, she immediately filed for divorce and moved out of the house, taking her live-in lover with her. Sam was devastated, then enraged. Although he finally forgave his ex-wife, he had no desire to reconcile with her. Fortunately, he didn't have to as part of the process of forgiving.

Min, on the other hand, did experience a reconciliation. Following a bitter dispute over the estate of their parents, Min and her sister had not spoken for more than a decade. Min's anger at her sister's behavior made communication impossible. When Min developed cancer, she forgave her sister as part of her new perspective on life. A reconciliation ensued, and they returned to the happier days of their youth. With forgiveness, reconciliation may take place, but it is not a requirement and will not come about unless we want it.

We Should Forgive Only If the Other Person Deserves It

Whether the persons who hurt us deserve our forgiveness has nothing to do with our decision to grant it. Their apologies or amends might make it easier for us to forgive them psychologically, but it isn't a requirement. We forgive for ourselves, not for the offending parties, so it doesn't matter whether they deserve it or not. The phrase "deserves to be forgiven" and its reverse "doesn't deserve to be forgiven" are such a part of the English language that we don't stop to consider whether "deserving" is a valid reason to withhold forgiveness. It isn't.

When Tom was thirteen, his father divorced his mother and remarried shortly thereafter. Desperate for his father's companionship and approval, Tom moved in with his father, stepmother, and three stepbrothers and stepsisters from his stepmother's first marriage. It quickly became clear that Tom would not be treated like the other children, like *her children*. He was denied the new clothes, the new bedroom furniture, and the electronic wonders that went to the others. More important, he was pointedly denied the praise, the approval, and the hugs that were given to his step siblings. Tom spent a miserable three years in his father's house, returning to his mother when he was sixteen. His father kept promising him love, affection, and good times, but he never delivered them. Tom finally forgave his father for the brutal emotional treatment of his adolescent years but not because his father deserved it. Tom did it because *he* deserved it, because he wanted to be free of that regret and the pain it caused him.

We Only Forgive in Response to a Request for It

No request from the offending party is necessary for our forgiveness. It is *we* who ask ourselves to forgive the other person, and it is *we* who benefit most from that forgiving. It doesn't matter whether the offending parties ask us to forgive them or not. In fact, some of the parties who hurt us may never know we have forgiven them. Or care. Others may be dead and incapable of asking for forgiveness. When Erek married a woman whom his parents disapproved of, they disinherited him and refused to see him or his family again. They took that commitment to the grave, having never seen their grandchildren. Erek forgave them even before their deaths, but they never asked for that forgiveness, nor were they particularly interested in receiving it.

If We Forgive, We Are Being Disloyal to Those the Offending Party Hurt in Addition to Ourselves

This misconception is a culmination of the preceding myths, which hold that forgiveness means having to forget or excuse offending behavior, reconcile with the offender, release the offender from accountability, or judge the offender deserving of forgiveness. Not one of the foregoing myths is true, yet they are all part, in one way or another, of the myth that forgiving is an act of disloyalty to the people the offending party hurt.

Margarita's child was abducted while playing in the front yard and later killed by an itinerant with mental problems. At first, Margarita was unable to forgive. Then the hatred began to consume her. As she sought to forgive, she feared that forgiving the killer might be an act of disloyalty to her child. Gradually, Margarita came to see that the reverse was true. She was confident that her child wanted her to be happy, free of the hatred that was devouring her, and released from the agony of focusing on her child's violent death. The route to that objective was through forgiveness, so Margarita came to believe that forgiveness was what her child would want for her. Margarita's friends did not agree that she should forgive the killer and aggressively or subtly tried to dissuade her. But Margarita persisted, convinced that she had an ally in her child and that she must forgive if she were to find peace. Margarita did ultimately forgive the killer. She also found release from the hatred and freedom from the torment.

We Forgive Only on the Basis of Certain Conditions Such as Getting an Apology

Forgiveness is unconditional or it is not forgiveness. If we make our forgiveness conditional on what the other party does, such as apologizing, we have made the perpetrator the decision maker in our process of forgiving. Ironically, we have turned our lives over to the very person who has hurt us, to the very one we resent or hate.

Those who don't understand the purpose of forgiveness often demand an apology as a condition that has to be met for them to forgive. But no apology is necessary. Requiring an apology implies that the offending party can "earn" our forgiveness through an apology. But forgiveness is always freely given. We give it for ourselves, not for the benefit of the offending party. Forgiveness *can* be granted for the sake of others as well as for our own sake, but it is primarily granted because of its positive effect on the quality of our own life. Even in those cases where we continue to be injured and there is never an apology, we can still forgive.

Hiroshi was in business with two co-owners who reneged on their promises, took advantage of her trusting nature, and legally cornered her. Until she could exit the business, however, she had to deal with them or lose everything. In desperation, she forgave them even though they had not changed their behavior or apologized for it. She no longer trusted them or liked them, but she could now deal with them in order to protect her own financial interests.

Forgiveness Isn't Valid Unless It Is Accepted by the Other Party

This myth is reinforced by the common phrase, "to offer our forgiveness," as if forgiveness had to be accepted to be valid. Forgiveness is not offered. It's granted. It is our gift to ourselves. It doesn't matter whether the other party accepts the gift. It is the giving that counts. If acceptance of forgiveness were a criterion for its validity, other people could keep us from forgiving. They can't. Forgiveness is never conditional. Forgiveness cannot be conditional and be forgiveness.

Once we get beyond these myths, we realize how important forgiveness is, even when it's very difficult. Our goal should be to forgive dangerously, as Mariah Burton Nelson has written in her splendid book *The Unburdened Heart.*

Letting Go of Resentments

In Step Two, you listed the people you still blame for your regrets. These are the people against whom you hold resentments because of those regrets. Resentments are a form of hatred. They are characterized by continuing anger at somebody or something for real or imagined offenses. Unfortunately, hatred in whatever form is binding, which means that you are inevitably tied to that which you hate. You are never free in hating but always trapped.

A simple test will prove it. Think of something someone did to you that you didn't like. Perhaps she slighted you, threatened you, or humiliated you. Notice how quickly your state of mind changes: from happy, serene, or satisfied to unhappy, disturbed, or angry. In the moment you returned to the resentment and felt its anger, your mood changed. Ironically, you just turned your emotional state over to the very person who harmed you. It was the thought of that person's action that took charge of your emotions and altered your mood. The person you despise just took control of your feelings.

With every resentment, we are victimized again by the person we loathe. Except that we are no longer the victim. We are the perpetrator. We have invited that person back from the past to inhabit our present, and once again we have given him or her control over our emotions and, thus, over the quality of our life. We have created a ghost and invited it back to hurt us again, asking the offending person to join us in the present to do one more time what he or she did to us in the past. There is a difference, however. This time, we are responsible for the pain the offender inflicts.

Resentments create a pool of anger in our lives that we can tap at will to distract us from other emotions, such as fear or pain, or to give us strength and energy when we want it. We summon that anger and fuel our resentments by returning repeatedly to the regrets that spawned those resentments, thinking about them, and getting angry all over again. In some cases, resentments born of regrets are so intense that they turn into thoughts of revenge or plans for revenge, whether or not we act on them. The desire for reprisals, paybacks, and vengeance against those who have hurt us is a tasty sweet. But it has a bitter aftertaste and destructive side effects. When revenge steals our mind, it drains energy from productive purposes and distracts us with counterproductive fantasies. When revenge becomes a preoccupation, it throws us into a constant state of turmoil, derails our lives, and excludes us from the pleasures of the present. In its extreme form, revenge becomes an obsession that sentences us to a desperate life of plotting and rage, exposing us to serious, even life-threatening consequences.

Resentments and thoughts of revenge are sustained by our refusal to forgive. They are deeply corrosive and preclude a rich and happy life. They also bind us to our regrets. To let go of a regret, we have to let go of the resentments that help maintain it.

Working the Step

Over the previous seven steps, you have examined your regrets, grieved your losses, acknowledged responsibility for your actions, and made amends. You have identified the lessons and gifts of your regrets, explored and neutralized the toxic thought patterns that have tied you to them, and developed compassion for yourself, recognizing that your past behavior was the best you could manage at the time. All that remains in the process of letting go of your regrets is forgiveness.

In Step Eight, you will forgive those who have harmed you. If your regrets do not involve being hurt by someone, and you hold no resentments against anyone or anything in connection with your regrets, this step is not necessary. But if there are other parties to your regrets whom you blame for at least some of what happened, this step is critical.

The following Action List will guide you through Step Eight:

Action List: Step Eight

Forgiving Others

1. List the people to forgive
2. Reasons your forgiveness is needed
3. Benefits of forgiving
4. Reasons for not forgiving
5. The act of forgiveness

Complete the Action List for each of your regrets in accordance with the following guidelines. Use the spiritual and psychological tools to overcome any resistance you encounter to forgiving each of the people you blame for your regret or against whom you hold any kind of resentment.

I. List the People to Forgive

Return to your journaling exercise for Step Two ("Examining Regrets") and reread the list of people whom you still blame for your regrets. Most of the people you need to forgive will be on this list. Identify anyone else connected with your regrets whom you still resent, blame, or hate. This is your forgiveness list.

2. Reasons Your Forgiveness Is Needed

In this activity, describe what each person on your forgiveness list has done to hurt you, and, hence, why you hate, blame, or resent him or her. In other words, for what must you forgive each person on the list for your forgiveness to be complete?

3. Benefits of Forgiving

Review the benefits of forgiving described earlier in this chapter. Which of these benefits would you reap from forgiving each person on your forgiveness list? What other benefits can you list that you would receive from forgiving each of these people? Understanding these benefits and writing them down will help you overcome any resistance that you might have to forgiving these people and remind you that you forgive not for them but for yourself.

4. Reasons for Not Forgiving

Examine the reasons you have for not granting complete and unconditional forgiveness to each person on your forgiveness list. The myths of forgiveness may help you in identifying some of these reasons. Use thought analysis and other spiritual and psychological tools to counteract these reasons after you have identified them.

If you are still unwilling to forgive, the following journaling activity will help you uncover additional reasons you have for withholding forgiveness. For this exercise, first identify each person on your forgiveness list whom you are still unwilling to forgive. Then complete the following sentence for each of these individuals, inserting his or her name, and finishing the sentence with whatever reason comes to mind:

I would forgive you, (name) , except that _____.

If you are still resistant to forgiving after completing this sentence, repeat the exercise with the next reason that comes to mind. Continue the process until you run out of reasons for not forgiving this person.

When you have journaled in this way about every person whom you are unwilling to forgive, you will have identified your reasons for withholding forgiveness. Now you can use thought analysis and the other spiritual and psychological tools to overcome them and to find the willingness you need. In addition, you may want to use two other techniques to help you forgive. These are described in the following paragraphs.

Developing Compassion for Others

If you are having trouble forgiving someone, try to develop compassion for that person just as you did for yourself in Step Seven. In that step, you accepted that you had done the best you could, given who you were at the time of the regret and the circumstances that existed then. In reaching some understanding of why you behaved as you did, you prepared yourself for developing a similar understanding of how others might have behaved as they did in creating or adding to the regret that now burdens you. After all, they, like you, may have done the best they could, given the circumstances that existed at the time and their own psychological and spiritual condition.

Of course, you cannot read the minds of other people, and you will never know what really motivated them. In the case of brutality, random violence, or sexual abuse, it is hard to feel compassion, because the offense is so outside our understanding. You can, however, appreciate that something went terribly wrong in the offender's life. It is possible to develop compassion without knowing the specific reasons for the offending party's unacceptable behavior. For example, you can appreciate, intellectually, that there had to be difficulties, struggles, and defects of character that led to the unacceptable actions, or they would not have taken place.

Alcoholic parents are an example. Compassion does not excuse their alcoholic behavior –either their abusive acts while drinking or their failure to get into recovery. It does not justify their actions, condone their behavior, or absolve them of accountability, but it may explain some of what they did. You will never know the real reasons for their behavior, of course, unless they tell you, and even they may not know. You cannot know the details, but you can grasp that they were troubled souls whose behavior was destructive and unacceptable, very likely to them as well as to you.

Compassion is sometimes facilitated by working to accept that the offending party's behavior was more about them than it was about us. In fact, in some cases, it may not have been about us at all even though we were the objects of that behavior or were directly affected. When innocent bystanders are victims in a tragic accident or children are brutalized, they are never at fault. When family members are the offending parties, we may have to develop compassion for what they *could not do* as much as for what they *did not do.* Their terrible limitations, which were so hurtful to us, were ultimately about them and their lives, even though they involved us. It may be that the limitations of our parents or siblings and their destructive behavior have affected us terribly, but their actions were still mostly about them.

None of this, of course, means that we have to approve of the offending parties' behavior, excuse it, or minimize it. It does mean, however, that we can try to understand their behavior as a projection of their personality and problems, which may lead us to enough compassion to make forgiving them easier.

The Healing Letter

A healing letter sent to those who have harmed you will help you forgive. This tool can be as effective in Step Eight as it was in Step Five, although the nature of the healing letter will be somewhat different. Its purpose in this step is to allow you to confront the person who harmed you and hold him or her accountable. You will detail the painful facts of your relationship so that you can let the pain of that relationship go. It doesn't matter whether the letter's recipient is living or dead. You can write anyone: parents who didn't nurture you, friends who betrayed you, business partners who cheated you, or spouses who abused you. You can even write to God, explaining how much the difficulties of your life have hurt and how unhappy you are to have had them.

The healing letter should be highly specific and emotionally laden. Its grammar and punctuation are unimportant, and you can even make a list of hurts if you wish. You can use drawings, poetry, pictures, photographs, collages or anything else that will convey what you need to say to this person but never had the chance to say. Cite detailed examples of the offending behavior. Describe the fear, the humiliation, or the torment you suffered. Describe the betrayal you felt, the unfairness of what happened, the futility of the things you tried to do to make the situation better. Write about your disappointments, the hopes you had, and what you lost. Describe the effect it had on your life. Recount the pain and the tears that overcame you on the worst of the days. Hold nothing back. This is your chance to say everything you have ever wanted to say to the recipient so that, finally, you can let it all out—and let it go. This letter is not an exercise in whining, self-pity, or victimization. It is the opposite. You are standing up for yourself and telling the truth. With everything said, you can move out of the past where this person holds sway into the present where the power is yours.

Toward the end of the letter, you may want to write—if it's true—how much you once liked or loved the person, how much he or she once meant to you, how grateful you are for the good times the two of you had. You can explain how those memories made everything that happened afterward all the more painful. If the other party did anything right or good, you may want to acknowledge that along with anything else you are grateful for from the relationship.

It might be well to conclude your healing letter by saying that you are going to forgive the recipient. Explain why you are forgiving the person and that your forgiveness does not excuse what he or she did. Explain that the forgiveness you're granting is for you but that it is nonetheless genuine. You no longer want to be tied to the past or to the world the two of you once inhabited together. So, by this letter, you are forgiving the person and setting yourself free.

One letter may be sufficient for your purposes, or it may take a dozen.

You will know when you have written everything you need to say. You will know when you have signed the last letter. It will be the letter that truly forgives the person and lets that person go.

5. The Act of Forgiveness

Forgiving is a psychological and spiritual process. It is psychological because it involves our thoughts and feelings, and because forgiving unconditionally is one of the most mature acts of which a human being is capable. Forgiveness means setting aside our self-centeredness and the immature part of us that demands vengeance and retribution in favor of the mature part that seeks freedom and peace. Ultimately, forgiveness is based on our acceptance of reality, our acknowledgment of life's imperfection, and our recognition that resentments and hatred hurt us most of all.

Forgiving is spiritual because it is a transcendent experience that reaches beyond the purely psychological, strategic, or rational. Forgiving draws upon the deepest and most profound part of us for its strength and purpose. It acknowledges love as the most powerful of human emotions— love of others and of ourselves. Forgiving expands our consciousness and introduces us to a larger world where forces beyond our understanding create miracles of change that sweep through us and others. In forgiving, we transcend the limitations of the material world to touch the infinite. In forgiving, we capture with our mind the freedom that our soul never relinquishes.

Once you have completed the activities for this step, ask yourself if you have forgiven all of the individuals on your forgiveness list. Have you released your anger, resentment, and hatred toward them? If so, for each person on your forgiveness list, write in your journal, "I have forgiven you, (name), for _____ (whatever you have forgiven him or her)." After writing each name, thank your higher power, however defined, for your willingness to forgive and for the help that made it possible. Conclude by asking your higher power to bless the person you have just forgiven. If you feel a sense of having forgiven the person, if you feel your anger released, and if you feel lighter of spirit, your forgiveness is complete.

If, for any reason, you want to tell the people on your list that you have forgiven them, you may do so in person, by telephone, or by letter. In the case of those who are deceased or unreachable, you can send them a healing letter if you have not already done so.

When Forgiveness Doesn't Come

If you do not want to write "I have forgiven you" for each of the people on your forgiveness list, continue to work on forgiving those you have chosen not to forgive at this time. Prepare another section in your journal titled "Tools of Forgiveness." For each of the unforgiven people on your list, develop a custom set of spiritual and psychological tools specifically designed to help you forgive that person. Then apply these tools daily until forgiveness comes. Include the following:

- Prayers for the willingness to forgive
- Prayers for the person you are seeking to forgive, asking that they might be blessed
- Affirmations of forgiving
- Visualizations of forgiving
- Journaling about your continuing resistance to forgiving this person

  In addition, use these tools regularly:
- Sharing with others, including your confidant, about those you have not forgiven
- Thought analysis, including the benefits of forgiving, the reasons to forgive, and the price of not forgiving
- Healing letters

Maintaining Forgiveness

Over time, some of the resentments you had against the people you have forgiven may creep back into your life. If so, you will feel less forgiving of those who have harmed you, especially if some form of interaction with them is still required. Do not be discouraged. You can grant forgiveness and retract it many times before it becomes a permanent condition. But each time you forgive, it will be easier, until it finally becomes such a natural part of your life that you will do it quickly and, generally, with little effort.

If a permanent state of forgiveness for someone seems to take a long time to achieve, be patient. If you have forgiven once, you can forgive again. Forgiveness is a process, which means that you may sometimes slip back into your old ways of thinking and behaving even as you are developing new ways. Return to this step if your resentments come back. Review what you have written and use the same exercises to reforgive. The road to forgiving may be long or short, bumpy or smooth. But it is a rich and rewarding road that leads to the greatest of treasures: freedom and love.

12

Step Nine: Forgiving Ourselves

The door to freedom from regret is open.

Will you walk through it?

Step Nine brings you to the threshold of accomplishment, to the time of letting go of your regrets. All the effort you have expended since reading the first page of this book has prepared you for this step, the step of freedom. In the ninth step, you will forgive yourself for whatever role you played in creating and maintaining your regrets. Then you will let go of those regrets to leave the pain of the past behind and step boldly into the present with all its possibilities.

Letting go of your regrets is by made possible by self-forgiveness. The model in Step Eight that worked for forgiving other people applies equally well to forgiving ourselves. There are two important distinctions, however. In self-forgiving, we are both the grantor and the recipient of our forgiveness. The second distinction is that with self-forgiveness, as opposed to forgiving others, reconciliation always occurs. In fact, that is one of its goals. Through self-forgiveness, we will experience the deep joy of reconciliation with ourselves that comes from both forgiving and *being forgiven*. In self-forgiveness, we are reunited with ourselves and so experience profound healing. Like all forgiveness, self-forgiveness is an act of love and a gift of the spirit that comes back to us many times over. When we have forgiven ourselves, we feel right with the world. We have no apologies to make, nothing about which to feel guilty, and nothing of which to be ashamed. We are free.

Self-forgiveness is essential to letting go of regrets. No matter how many times we have forgiven others or others have forgiven us for the regrets we hold, we will not be truly free until we have forgiven ourselves. Even if others have not forgiven us, however, we will still find the same freedom in our self-forgiveness.

One of the myths associated with self-forgiveness is that we can only forgive ourselves after those we have harmed have forgiven us. That is not the case. Self-forgiveness is the peace we make with ourselves and with God, however we understand God. It is not the peace we make with others. It does not depend, therefore, on anyone else. Through our amends we have already made peace with the other parties to our regret. It doesn't matter whether they have made peace with us. It does not matter whether they have forgiven us. We do not need their permission or approval to forgive ourselves. Forgiveness is our gift, one we make to ourselves. We don't need anyone else's permission to make that gift.

In the final analysis, self-forgiveness is an act of compassion, an acknowledgment of our imperfections, and an expression of our humility. It is giving ourselves permission to be who we were—and who we are.

The Benefits of Forgiving Ourselves

Just as we reap benefits from forgiving others, we reap benefits from forgiving ourselves. These benefits are the primary reasons we forgive. They are the fruits of having let go of our regrets, the gifts we receive for the progress we have made, the fear we have overcome, and the courage we have shown. They are well deserved.

Self-forgiveness is warranted on the basis of three sets of principles: intellectual, psychological, and spiritual. Intellectually, self-forgiveness is the most rational and practical policy we can pursue if we wish to lead a happy and productive life. Psychologically, it frees us from the bonds of self-loathing that cripple our relationships with ourselves and others, impairing our ability to fulfill our potential. Spiritually, self-forgiveness is an act of love and an example of grace that spreads throughout our relationships and activities, bringing multiple gifts to us and to others.

We forgive ourselves for many reasons, some of which include the following:

Self-Forgiveness Is an Act of Love and Compassion

Withholding forgiveness is an act of hate. Forgiving is an act of love. If we refuse to forgive ourselves, that refusal is an expression of self-hatred. Hatred is no basis for the relationship we have with ourselves, which is as real as any relationship we have with another human being. Because we are always with ourselves, the self-forgiveness we withhold is even more destructive than the forgiveness we withhold from others. As an act of compassion and expression of love toward ourselves, self-forgiveness benefits us profoundly. It frees us from the internal hostilities that regrets impose. It also brings us an extraordinary gift: the joy of loving and of being loved, perhaps the most healing of all human experiences.

Self-Forgiveness Allows Us to Live in the Present

With each regret, we return to the past and to the events that made us unhappy there. We re-create the misery of yesterday and bring it into our present lives to poison them. Every moment we spend in our regrets deprives us of a moment in the present that we might otherwise have enjoyed. Self-forgiveness returns us to the present where we belong, where we were meant to live, and where the pleasures of life can be experienced.

Self-Forgiveness Frees Us of the Shame and Guilt of Our Regrets

For those regrets about which we feel guilt or shame, self-forgiveness is wonderfully freeing. It allows us to shed the painful past. Regardless of how well publicized our regret has been, we no longer have to fear what people will think of us or to shrink from them in spasms of guilt or shame. We have made our amends. We are right with ourselves, with our higher power, and with the world. The harsh judgments of others are no longer of consequence. Their thoughts are theirs to handle and resolve. Forgiveness frees us from whatever we have done in the past to do whatever we need to do in the present to enjoy our lives and make them meaningful and successful.

Self-Forgiveness Makes Possible a Deep Sense of Peace and Even Happiness

Peace, serenity, and enduring happiness elude us as long as we are punishing ourselves with regrets. When we live in self-blame and self-directed anger, we cannot be at peace with ourselves, which means that we cannot be happy. Self-forgiveness brings an end to the self-punishment of regretting and to the turmoil it causes, ushering in a new era of self-acceptance, self-respect, and expanded opportunities. Once we have forgiven ourselves, we are free to enjoy ourselves, to experience our own unique expression of life with all its hopes and possibilities.

Self-Forgiveness Makes It More Likely That We Will Continue to Forgive Others

When we have not forgiven ourselves, it is more difficult to forgive others in the daily conduct of our lives. Forgiving ourselves provides practice in the art of forgiving other people. The better we are at self-forgiveness, the better we will understand the process of forgiving others and the rewards it brings. Likewise, the more practiced we are at forgiving others, the easier it will be to forgive ourselves when new reasons arise to do so, as they inevitably will.

Self-Forgiveness Makes It More Likely That We Will Not Take Back the Forgiveness We Have Granted Others

If we continue to blame ourselves for our regrets, we may become resentful of the forgiveness we have granted others. That we have forgiven them and not ourselves seems unfair, and it is. Why should we suffer while they go free? If we do not forgive ourselves, we may retract the forgiveness we have granted others, reblaming the parties to our regrets for their actions and slowly withdrawing our forgiveness. Should that happen, we have begun to reconstruct our regrets and slowly but surely, to work our way backward through the steps. Self-forgiveness is one means by which we guard against this possible retreat.

Self-Forgiveness Heals Our Relationship with Ourselves and So with Others

It is difficult to have a bitter relationship with oneself and a loving relationship with other people. The two sets of relationships are too intimately related. It's as if they draw from a common pool of love that is either expanding or contracting, depending upon our willingness to forgive. When we are in a state of unforgiveness—of self-criticism, self-denunciation, and self-hatred—we have less love for ourselves or other people. Through self-forgiveness—an act of love—we increase our reservoir of love to share with others and, ironically, with ourselves. Out of such love meaningful relationships are created, maintained, and expanded, and our lives grow richer.

When we are continually blaming ourselves for our regrets, living in emotional self-flagellation, or brutalizing ourselves for our mistakes, we tend to isolate emotionally. With self-forgiveness, we rejoin the world emotionally and experience community. We welcome ourselves back to participate as worthy equals in the remarkable journey of life. The terrible sense of isolation spawned by our regrets—the wall that separates us from ourselves and others—falls away. We never have to feel alone again.

Self-Forgiveness Is Required for Letting Go of Our Regrets

As long as we withhold self-forgiveness for the part we played in our regrets, we will remain tied to them, and they will continue to exercise their dark influence over us. Only through forgiving ourselves can we finally release those regrets. Self-forgiveness is the last act of letting go, but it is mandatory. Without it, we will remain trapped in our regrets. Without self-forgiveness, we cannot be free.

Myths of Self-Forgiveness:
What Forgiving Ourselves Is Not

Just as there are myths about what it means to forgive others, there are myths about what it means to forgive oneself. These myths distort our understanding of self-forgiveness, how it works, and what it is designed to achieve. When these myths find their way into our thinking as reasons for withholding self-forgiveness, they block us from forgiving ourselves and keep us tied to our regrets. Some of the myths about self-forgiveness are closely related to the myths about forgiving others. Some of the most common myths about self-forgiveness are described in the following paragraphs.

If I Forgive Myself, I Will Be Excusing My Behavior

Self-forgiveness does not excuse or condone our inappropriate behavior in any way. Even as we forgive ourselves, we hold ourselves accountable for our part in the regret and for its consequences. But we have accepted responsibility and made amends for our actions, and we can do no more. Further punishment serves no useful purpose. We have satisfied our debt. While not excusing our behavior, we accept it as part of who we were at the time. We can remain forever accountable for what we have done and still forgive ourselves.

If I Forgive Myself, I Will Be More Likely to Repeat the Same Behavior

This myth assumes that continuous self-punishment is the only way to keep our renegade selves under control or that if we forgive ourselves, we will somehow forget what we did and repeat it. Forgiveness does not mean denying or forgetting our past actions, however, nor does it mean that we will no longer hold ourselves accountable for what we have done. Self-forgiveness comes after we have acknowledged our inappropriate behavior, made amends for it, and changed our behavior to prevent a recurrence, all of which provide protection against repeating it.

I Can Forgive Myself Only If I Have Met Specific Conditions

As with all forgiveness, self-forgiveness is unconditional. Forgiveness is freely given to ourselves, because we are one more person on the list of people to forgive if we want to let go of our regrets. We can't establish conditions for forgiving ourselves any more than we can establish conditions for forgiving someone else.

In practical terms, however, we will have met certain conditions. The first eight steps fulfill the psychological and spiritual conditions that will make us comfortable forgiving ourselves, including having made amends. Even so, our actions in the first eight steps have not "earned" our self-forgiveness, which is still freely given, without conditions.

I Can't Forgive Myself Because I Don't Deserve to Be Forgiven

Forgiving ourselves has nothing to do with deserving forgiveness. When we forgive ourselves, we do so as the *grantor* of that forgiveness, not because we are its *recipient.* We forgive ourselves for the same reason we forgave people in Step Eight without questioning whether they "deserved" it. We have to forgive ourselves to let go of our regrets. From a practical standpoint, once we have made our apologies and reparations and have changed our behavior, there is nothing more we could possibly do to "deserve" forgiveness. But even if we had done none of that, forgiveness would still be ours to give.

We forgive ourselves to reap the same benefits as grantor that we got from forgiving other people. We forgive because we cannot be as productive, generous, or compassionate when we fail to forgive ourselves as when we do. Rationally, we cannot forgive the other parties to our regret and yet withhold forgiveness from ourselves, because our objective in forgiving is the same with every person involved in the regret. In this case, we happen to be the recipient of the forgiveness as well as the grantor of it. But that dual role is irrelevant to the decision to forgive ourselves.

Some people feel they don't "deserve" to be forgiven because they don't think they have been punished enough for their actions. Why should they be let off the hook, they ask themselves? Because self-forgiveness is not determined by how much we have been punished any more than forgiving others is determined by how much they have been punished. Forgiveness is unconditional. It has nothing to do with punishment. It is given in response to our own needs, as grantor, not as the result of "sufficient punishment" administered to ourselves or anyone else.

I Am Unable to Forgive Myself

Regardless of claims made to the contrary, no one is incapable of self-forgiveness. If we refuse to forgive ourselves by the time we have reached Step Nine, it is because we have *chosen* not to forgive ourselves. We are still indulging some toxic thought pattern that prevents us from forgiving. Self-forgiveness is a choice, just as forgiving others is a choice—a choice we always have the power to make.

I Am Not Entitled to Forgive Myself; Only the Other Party Can

Some people claim that we have an inherent conflict of interest as both the grantor and the recipient of forgiveness that makes self-forgiveness theoretically impossible. According to this view, we are not sufficiently objective to forgive ourselves, so we must depend on others for that forgiveness. This myth, like many others, is based on a misunderstanding of the meaning of forgiveness and, especially, of self-forgiveness. All forgiveness is the same in nature whether it is granted to others or to ourselves: it is unconditional.

Forgiveness is never given or withheld as if it were a legal decision reached in a court of law, based on the logic of arguments and counterarguments traded and then somberly considered. Neither is forgiveness granted on the basis of conditions negotiated by the parties. Forgiveness of self and others is offered freely and unconditionally for all the reasons we have considered, or it is not forgiveness. Forgiveness is a gift of the spirit. Whether we "should" be forgiven on the basis of objective criteria is not relevant. Forgiveness is not based on the judgment we pass but on the love we give. We are as entitled to forgive ourselves as we are to forgive any other human being. The decision is ours alone to make.

People Will Criticize Me If I Forgive Myself

Perhaps, but other people will criticize you if you don't forgive yourself. People criticize people; it's part of being alive. If you base your life on what others think of you and refuse to do the things that are right and best for you because of the possibility of criticism, you will always be victimized and disappointed. Your life will be constructed on the complaints of others rather than on the dreams you have for yourself. Those who criticize you for self-forgiveness have neither the understanding of forgiveness nor the knowledge of your life necessary to render the judgment they make.

Working Step Nine

The process for working Step Nine is similar to the process used in working Step Eight since both steps involve granting forgiveness. Step Nine includes examining your need for self-forgiveness, identifying the benefits of self-forgiveness, analyzing any resistance you may have to self-forgiveness, overcoming your resistance to self-forgiveness, and forgiving yourself for your regrets.

The following Action List will guide you through Step Nine:

Action List: Step Nine

Forgiving Ourselves

1. Why I need to forgive myself
2. Reasons to forgive myself
3. Reasons for not forgiving myself
4. Overcoming resistance to forgiving myself
5. The act of forgiving myself
6. Letting go of your regrets

Complete the activities on the Action List for every regret for which you have not yet forgiven yourself. Here are the guidelines for those activities:

1. Why I Need to Forgive Myself

Describe the specific actions related to your regrets for which you need to forgive yourself. As was the case with forgiving others, self-forgiveness is granted for specified behavior. A blanket statement of forgiveness is not as effective as forgiveness for specific actions, because it is not as believable. The phrase "I forgive myself for everything" does not convey the power of "I forgive myself for abandoning my children and for all the pain I caused them, including their impoverished childhood." But even that statement may be too general. Approach the activity in this way: Pretend that you are coming to yourself as if you were a third party to ask forgiveness for your actions. What forgiveness would you specifically seek? You will intuitively know how much detail to include in your journal to be sure that your forgiveness feels complete.

Take Janet, for example, who became pregnant in high school and gave up her baby for adoption when the father refused to marry her. In her late twenties, she did marry, only to find that she could no longer have children. The longing for a child by the husband she loved intensified her regret at having given away the only child she would ever bear. In a hell of self-hatred and remorse, she returns to that decision over and over. "If only . . ." Trapped in the past, she won't forgive herself for the choice she made as an adolescent and so can't find her way to the present where happiness awaits her. Yet the forgiveness she seeks, but says she cannot have, is hers to give.

Diego regretted the cruel way he treated his parents for decades as he struggled to find maturity and balance in his life. Now that he is mature, they are dead, and he deeply regrets the opportunities he missed with them and the pain he caused them. He continues to punish himself with memories of what might have been.

2. Reasons to Forgive Myself

In this journaling activity, develop a list of reasons to forgive yourself for your role in the regrets you harbor. Review the benefits of self-forgiveness that were described earlier in this chapter and apply them to your own re-grets. Think deeply on the difference it would make in the quality of your life if you were to forgive yourself and find release from the pain and suffering of the regrets that bind you to the past. Be comprehensive and thorough, because this list provides the primary motivation for letting go of your regrets.

In the final analysis, the best reason for forgiving ourselves may be that we were meant to forgive ourselves. Life drives us toward self-forgiveness. When we do not forgive ourselves, we will be tormented by the past and its regrets. The unwarranted and unnecessary pain of those regrets thwarts our spiritual growth and psychological development and serves no beneficial purpose. We do not have to endure it. We are not asked to endure it. In fact, life calls us to do the opposite: to let it go, to forgive.

3. Reasons for Not Forgiving Myself

If you are ready to forgive yourself, this journaling activity will not be necessary. If, on the other hand, you still feel resistance, you will find it helpful. In this exercise, you will seek the reasons that block your self-forgiveness. Begin by asking yourself, "What is holding me back? Why am I unwilling to forgive myself?" Some of these reasons may be based on the myths of self-forgiveness described earlier in the chapter. Toxic thought patterns that prevent self-forgiveness may also be culprits. Explore all these possibilities to discover potential reasons.

If you are still hesitant to forgive yourself, try this exercise to uncover more reasons. Start with a clean page in your journal. On the left-hand side of the page, write the phrase "I forgive myself for _____," inserting the name of the regret for which you are unwilling to forgive yourself. As you write the sentence, you may feel resistance to forgiving yourself. If so, an objection will come to mind. This objection is an unresolved reason you have for not wanting to forgive yourself. Write it down.

Repeat this process as long as a new reason comes to mind. When the objections start to repeat themselves, or when you no longer feel resistant to forgiving yourself, you have completed the activity for this regret.

4. Overcoming Resistance to Forgiving Myself

If you are now ready to forgive yourself for each of your regrets, this action item can be omitted. If you are not yet ready, use the spiritual and psychological tools to help you find the willingness you need. For example, pray for that willingness and for the courage to forgive yourself. Ask your higher power to help you understand why forgiving yourself is warranted, why it is important for you to do so, and why you are resisting it. Pray for the power to let go of the self-blaming, anger, and hatred that keep you from self-forgiveness. Ask your higher power to lead you to self-forgiveness in whatever ways would be best for you.

Use thought analysis to determine the reasons for your unwillingness to forgive yourself and then develop logical arguments to counter those reasons.

Use creative visualization to imagine what it would feel like to forgive yourself, including all of the benefits you would receive. Feel the self-blame and the anger over your regrets fade away, your guilt and shame recede, your fear and unhappiness disappear. See yourself as forgiven. Visualize having completed Step Nine with a sense of release, accomplishment, and happiness.

Use affirmations to overcome resistance. Affirm "I forgive myself" or "I am forgiven," feeling the power of the words as you utter them.

Confirmation of Divine Forgiveness

For many spiritual people, self-forgiveness is only possible in conjunction with the forgiveness of their higher power, however they define that power. Any attempt to forgive themselves that excluded divine forgiveness would be meaningless. Therefore, for such people, the process of self-forgiveness includes seeking God's forgiveness and then accepting that God has forgiven them. If the forgiveness of your higher power is an important part of forgiving yourself, do whatever you need to do in order to obtain or confirm that forgiveness, given your concept of the higher power. If you require a formal religious rite to bestow or confirm God's forgiveness, seek a priest, minister, rabbi, or other member of the clergy who can forgive you in the name of God.

5. The Act of Forgiving Myself

When you are ready to forgive yourself, you may intuitively know how to do it in a way that is meaningful and convincing to you. Or you may not. Ordinarily, the most effective acts of self-forgiveness involve some kind of ritual. A ritual is a ceremonial act that marks a significant transition. Religious rituals, such as confirmations and bar mitzvahs, symbolize the transition from childhood to young adulthood. Presidential inaugurations symbolize the orderly transfer of political and military power. Birthdays symbolize the passage of another year of life. Rituals confirm to the participants and to others that a noteworthy, even momentous, event has occurred. They validate that something about our lives is different. Because of the symbolic power of rituals to confirm that change has taken place, they can be an important element in self-forgiveness.

There is no best way to forgive yourself. A simple statement such as "I forgive myself for . . ." may be sufficient. Many people, however, prefer something more elaborate and more dramatic to symbolize their self-forgiveness and to create a vivid and convincing memory. They prefer some kind of ritual. The design of the ritualistic act of self-forgiveness is up to you, because you are best qualified to determine what would be most persuasive, emotionally and spiritually. The ritual can be brief or lengthy, simple or elaborate, conducted alone or with others, depending upon what works best for you. Whatever its design, however, the ritual should relate to all of your regrets and all of their consequences. The act of self-forgiveness should be complete.

You may wish to conduct your ritual in a sacred place or a site that is special to you. You may want to include other people, such as your confidant, or you may prefer to be alone. You may even choose to have the ritual conducted by a clergyperson in a church or temple in accordance with your religious tradition. You may want to choose a ritualistic act that represents healing and freedom, which are gifts of self-forgiveness. The right design is one that feels comfortable to you and personally meaningful.

Beth designed her ritual of self-forgiveness around a park where she had spent many happy hours as a child playing in the woods and romping in the stream. As she thought about what she wanted from her act of self-forgiveness, she realized that it was to be cleansed of her regrets. She wanted them washed away; she wanted to start over with a clean slate and a new life. To symbolize that goal, Beth returned to the shallow stream where she had splashed as a child, submerging herself in its cool running water. She sat on a rock in the stream, letting the water gently wash past her, relaxing her body, and breathing the cool air of the woods. She went over each of the regrets and consequences for which she wanted to be forgiven, granting herself that forgiveness. She imagined herself accepting the forgiveness, felt herself free, and concluded with a prayer.

Beth stood up, feeling the guilt, shame, and blame of her regrets run off her body like the water itself, with whatever was left evaporating quickly in the afternoon sun. To Beth, the water represented the cleansing power of self-forgiveness and evaporation represented the loss of pain, guilt, and shame. Beth walked across the stream to the other side, which, to her, symbolized her passage to a new life without regrets. She stepped onto the bank, said a prayer of gratitude, and looked back once. Then she went off to a day devoted to doing things she enjoyed.

Luisa's ritual of self-forgiveness took place in a church, where she knelt before the altar and opened a small box containing a cross she had brought for this purpose. She raised the cross before the altar, asked God to bless it, and reconfirmed God's forgiveness of the actions that had created her regret. Then she put the cross around her neck and whispered "I forgive myself for . . . ," and she enumerated everything related to her regrets for which she wanted to be forgiven. She concluded with a final "I am forgiven." Luisa continued to wear the cross, and whenever she had an inclination to regret, she touched it.

Whether your ritual is conducted quietly at home or with friends in a special place, it should be deeply meaningful. You are offering yourself a priceless gift that you are, at the same time, accepting. This is the gift of love. It is the gift of forgiveness. It is the gift of freedom. The moment of your self-forgiving is sacred, because it will mean a reconciliation with yourself, a resolution of the strife within you, and an end to the self-attack and condemnation of your regrets. It will be a moment of freedom to be savored and cherished, breathed in like strong sea air.

Once your ritual of self-forgiveness has been completed, you are forgiven. For some people, this state of forgiveness is permanent. They feel profoundly the forgiveness they have offered themselves, and they accept it completely. They feel absolved of shame and guilt and enter into a new world of freedom and quiet happiness. Susan felt a sense of exhilaration when she completed her ritual of forgiveness. She felt free of the burden of self-hate and blaming that she had experienced for years over the death of her sister in a car she was driving. She felt reconciled with herself and her late sister, and she was at peace. She never went back to the blaming and the self-directed anger that had marred her life for years.

Pete also felt free after his ritual. As the days passed, however, the old habits of blaming and condemning himself returned. Gradually he lost the sense of forgiveness he had experienced and returned to a state of guilt and shame. When Pete realized what was happening, he went back to the steps. He reworked the eighth, ninth, and tenth steps and conducted another ritual of self-forgiveness. He was free again. Pete returned several more times to these steps and to his rituals before his self-forgiveness was complete. Self-forgiving was a longer process for Pete than for Susan. Nonetheless, in the end, he found the same relief and freedom from regret that she had. Each of Pete's returns to self-forgiveness was easier and longer lasting than the one before, building to the day when his self-forgiveness was permanent.

6. Letting Go of Your Regrets

Once you have forgiven yourself, there is nothing left to bind you to your regrets. You may find that they have already disappeared, like ghosts in the morning light. You may want to say a prayer of gratitude to acknowledge that disappearance. Or you may choose to reach for your journal, thumb its pages, and say, "These are the regrets I have let go. They will never hurt me again."

When you began your journey in chapter 1, the goal you set for yourself was to let go of your regrets and to find freedom from the pain of your past. With Step Nine, you have achieved that goal. The regrets that once burdened you have been released. Your success has not taken away the memory of those regrets, of course, but it has neutralized their power. You may remember your regrets for a lifetime, but their capacity to hurt you, to drag you back to the past, and to hold you hostage is gone. Old regrets will no longer distort your present or cause you pain. Each of them will become a tile in the mosaic of your life that was painful once, cost you dearly, and brought you gifts. You may still wish that you had never experienced the regrets—all their gifts and lessons notwithstanding—but you will no longer return to them. You will no longer dwell on them or inhabit the past from which they came. And they will no longer hurt you. In forgiving yourself and letting go of your regrets, you have reclaimed the present. You are free.

If you wish, a final ritual symbolizing letting go of your regrets can conclude Step Nine. As with self-forgiving, this ritual marks a significant transition in your life. And as with self-forgiving, the ritual can take many forms. The only requirement is that it be meaningful to you. Gabriela, for example, built a ceremony around her journal. She set the journal ablaze and watched the smoke rise in the afternoon sky and float away. She saw in the dissipating smoke all of her regrets and all of her sadness released to the heavens. She said a prayer of thanksgiving, asking to remain forever free of her regrets and thanking her higher power for the journey that had brought her to this moment. She chose an object to symbolize her letting go, a small charm she had discovered in an antiques store, which she held in her hand as the journal burned. She carried the charm with her for many months until she finally put it away in a secret place.

Brad chose not to burn his journal because he wanted to refer to it later should the need arise. Instead, on a single sheet of paper, he wrote down all of his regrets, the pain they had caused, and anything else associated with them that he wanted to release. He said a prayer of thanksgiving for his new freedom from regrets, asked for the courage to remain regret-free, and shredded the paper. He took the confetti of regrets and flushed it down the toilet, watching the paper swirl into the drain and disappear. Then he left with his confidant for dinner at his favorite restaurant, where he toasted his new life. Brad saved the matches from the restaurant as his symbolic object and left them on his dresser as a reminder of his new freedom.

Jaime found a stick like one of many he used to throw as a boy when he was teaching his dog to retrieve. He carved the word *Regrets* on the stick and took it to a bridge about an hour from his home. He stood on the bridge, pondering all the pain his regrets had caused him, and tossed the stick into the river below. As he watched it float away, he thought of it as carrying away all the guilt, shame, and remorse his regrets had caused him. This time, he said, the stick would not come back and neither would his regrets. He had let them go.

With the completion of Step Nine, you have forgiven yourself and let go of your regrets. There is a tenth step, however, because your newly won freedom from regret must be protected. In the next chapter, you will work that final step. It will keep you regret-free for the rest of your life.

13

STEP TEN: LIVING FREE OF REGRET

LIFE'S JOURNEY is not over until its end and, very likely, it isn't over then. Our own journey of letting go of our regrets has not ended, either. We have one more step to work—one for the many roads still to travel in the adventures of our life. Down all these roads, we want to travel regret-free, carrying neither old regrets that return nor fresh ones that we acquire. Of course, we can't avoid regretting. We're human. We're going to make mistakes that we regret, and things are going to happen to us that create regrets. But we need not carry them. We can use the Ten Steps to let them go.

Unlike the other nine steps, Step Ten is not about the past but about the eternal present in which we live our lives. Its purpose is to ensure that we neither return to our old regrets nor harbor new ones. When practiced daily, its tools and principles will keep us living firmly in the here and now and free of all regrets that would tie us to the past. Because the tenth step is about the present, it is the only step that we never complete and so never stop working.

Working the Step

The Action List for Step Ten consists of two categories of activities designed to keep you regret-free for the rest of your life. The first is a set of spiritual and psychological *principles* to apply daily. The second is regular application of the familiar spiritual and psychological *tools*, with special emphasis on thought analysis and prayer. The following paragraphs describe these activities in more detail.

Action List: Step Ten

Living Free of Regret

1. Apply the spiritual and psychological tools and principles to daily life

---

Apply the Spiritual and Psychological Tools and Principles to Daily Life

Throughout the steps, you have used a set of spiritual and psychological tools to let go of your regrets. Now you will use them to keep old regrets from returning and new regrets from staying with you. Each tool is effective, but you are likely to have favorites. The more tools you use and the more often you use them, the more effective you are likely to be with Step Ten. Develop the discipline to apply them quickly when the need arises. Pray for that discipline, visualize it, affirm it, and journal about it.

The following paragraphs describe how you can use the tools to stay free of regrets.

Thought Analysis

Thought analysis marshals the power of your rational mind to overcome unrealistic fears and fantasies and to reject invalid thoughts that would create new regrets or lead you back to old ones. Thought analysis served you well in letting go of your regrets, and it will continue to serve you well in keeping old regrets from reforming and new ones from staying with you. Each time you feel a regret returning, ask yourself which, if any, toxic thought pattern is re-creating it. When you identify the pattern, say to yourself something like "Ah-ha, another example of _____ [whatever toxic pattern it is]." Then address the specific characteristics of the pattern, and add "This thought isn't true and I will ignore it." For example, if the toxic thought pattern is exaggerated control, your response would be "Ah-ha, another example of exaggerated control. I don't have that kind of power. This thought is not true and I will ignore it." Use the same process on new regrets when you find yourself resistant to letting them go.

As we discussed in chapter 6, the most common toxic thought patterns that support regrets are:

- Perfectionism
- Exaggerated control
- Foreseeing the future
- Knowing what others are thinking
- Personalizing events
- Incomplete comparisons
- Undeserved guilt
- Reimagining the past
- Using regrets as justification for inaction

Prayer and Meditation

We are not meant to face the vicissitudes of life alone, without the guidance and support of our higher power. But we must ask for that support, draw on it, and accept it. Prayer is one means of doing that.

With dedicated practice, prayer will become one of the most rewarding activities of your life, bringing comfort, courage, strength, and peace in the midst of uncertainty and tumult. Fancy words are not required to pray. We don't have to pray to a prescribed concept of a higher power or have a great deal of faith to pray. Prayer works anyway.

People use prayer in many different ways. Some, for example, seek guidance in the morning for themselves as well as assistance for those they love. Others pray in the evening to offer thanks for the day's events. Still others pray throughout the day, whenever they need help, courage, or support—before giving a speech, meeting a deadline, or talking to an antagonist. By disciplining ourselves to commune with God in the quiet time of prayer, we renew our spirit and our strength, and we are granted the knowledge we need to function effectively in the world. Prayer heals, and we are healed by prayer. There is no substitute for prayer for those who seek a meaningful life.

Affirmations

You have used affirmations many times during your work on the Ten Steps and have already experienced their effectiveness. Whether said aloud before a mirror or silently through the day, affirmations implant in our minds the truth they contain. Affirmations directly counter the negative thoughts that we have repeated to ourselves for years, perhaps for a lifetime, that would resurrect old regrets or cause us to harbor new ones. For example, an old regret can be quelled when you are tempted to return to it by affirming "I have let that regret go. I am free." Or when old anger from past regrets arises, affirm to yourself "I have forgiven him (or her)."

Affirmations are effective against toxic thought patterns that would drive us to harbor new regrets. For example, if we are tempted to regret our failure to predict an outcome that would have changed our actions, we can remind ourselves, "My inability to predict the future is part of being human." We must counter the thoughts that shame, demean, or attack us if we are to become vibrant individuals growing and changing in positive ways. Affirmations are one way of doing that. They allow us to grow into and adopt new ways of thinking about ourselves and our situation by the simple means of affirming positive statements about them.

Creative Visualization

Creative visualization is a powerful way to facilitate change in your life. It can, for example, help you prepare for new opportunities that require you to take difficult, frightening, or even seemingly impossible actions. Skilled speakers know to imagine themselves speaking in front of their audience and hearing enthusiastic applause before they have entered the room to begin their speech. Great golfers imagine themselves with the perfect swing before they achieve it. To the mind, a carefully imagined scene filled with great detail is a convincing reality that approximates the power of an event that actually takes place. We can preexperience the things we need to do, fear to do, or want to do, so that we can prepare ourselves for them and handle them with greater ease, more competence, and less fear when we finally face them in real life.

Journaling

Not everyone likes to write. For those who have taken pleasure in keeping a journal or who have found relief in the written word, journaling may be an especially appropriate tool. Some people take to journaling quite naturally, but others do not. Even if it is not your preferred tool, however, you will nonetheless profit from it. Journaling is especially appropriate in situations driven by fear or confusion, because it sets limits on those fears and on that confusion, which is both clarifying and reassuring. Making a list of what you are afraid will happen is a powerful means of easing your anxieties.

Listing the pros and cons of a difficult decision and weighing each for its relative value will clarify your thought process and lead you intuitively to the best decision. Journaling is also an effective means of expressing and sorting through your feelings and your expectations. It complements thought analysis when you face new regrets and want to think them through. If the use of poetry or short stories or a visual journal in the form of drawings or collages was helpful in working previous steps, that form of journal will continue to serve you well with this step.

Sharing with Confidants

The need to share our lives with others never ends. We were meant to live not in isolation but in community. Friends help us explore the problems of our lives and find solutions. They share our joys and multiply them. They strengthen our courage and give us hope. Through friends, we find the support we need to grow spiritually and develop psychologically. Spiritual and emotional isolation are terrible burdens to bear, greater burdens than we were meant to carry. Regardless of how reserved we have been in our lives, we can learn to share ourselves with others and profit from that sharing if we work at it. The spiritual and psychological tools can help.

One place to start in learning to share with others is a small group that meets regularly. Many such groups exist, and a large proportion of the American population belongs to one. Small groups cover a diverse range of interests and vary considerably in sponsorship. They include sports teams, bridge clubs, book clubs, prayer groups, Bible study seminars, couples classes, Twelve-Step recovery groups (like Alcoholics Anonymous, Overeaters Anonymous, or Al-Anon), support groups that meet around a variety of illnesses and other problems, and a myriad of other groups that educate or provide emotional support. The defining characteristics of these groups are the sense of caring they offer their members and the opportunity to share about their lives in a place that feels safe. By joining one or more of these groups and attending regularly, you will develop friendships and be encouraged and inspired by the example of others to share some of your own life.

If sharing is intimidating for you, substantial courage may be required to do it. But you can pray for that courage, visualize it, affirm it, and journal about it. When you do, amazing things will happen. You will find extraordinary situations developing and extraordinary people appearing to assist you, people who have had similar experiences to yours and who have insights, strength, and hope to share. When you are trying to grow spiritually, you will be aided by powerful forces that work in unforeseen ways. That does not mean that your journey will be without fear, of course, but it does mean that you can tap the courage you need to overcome that fear. Sharing with others is one way to do that. The emotional, spiritual, and psychological support that friends and confidants provide will help you to remain regret-free.

Continue to Use the Ten Steps

Whenever an old regret threatens to come back or a new regret appears that is not easy to let go, return to the Ten Steps. Work whatever steps are required to release it. With many regrets, you will apply the steps you need quickly and intuitively. With more serious regrets, you may have to go back through the Ten Steps formally and deliberately. Regardless of the regret, you can let it go. The Ten Steps will always work for you.

Spiritual and Psychological Principles

In addition to the spiritual and psychological *tools*, you can employ a set of ten spiritual and psychological *principles* to keep old regrets from returning and to let go of new regrets. These principles are like the tools in that you apply them to remain regret-free. But they are different from the tools in that they are guides to effective living rather than specific techniques for changing your behavior. It could be said that the tools are the means to an end, whereas the principles are the ends you seek. The ten spiritual and psychological principles are:

1. Apply the lessons and gifts of your regrets.
2. Accept responsibility, make amends.
3. Stay grateful.
4. Practice humility.
5. Serve others.
6. Forgive yourself and others.
7. Accept others, accept life.
8. Reject old regrets.
9. Let go of new regrets.
10. Live resolutely in the present.

The following paragraphs will explore these principles in more detail.

Apply the Lessons and Gifts of Your Regrets

The lessons that your regrets have taught you and the gifts they have brought you have been costly and hard won. Yet to some degree, these lessons and gifts can make up for the pain of your regrets, if you are willing to recognize and use them. One way to profit from the lessons and gifts of your regrets is to apply them in your daily life. How to do that in order to benefit yourself and others is a question you will have to answer. Nicholas regretted squandering a sizable inheritance, but he came to terms with it and used the lessons of that regret to change his perspective on money and the way he handled it. He established a monthly budget, learned how to invest wisely, and taught his children the virtue of thrift. He also learned that "money isn't everything," as he once had thought it was, a gift he could also pass on to his children. Nicholas would rather have had the money he wasted than the lesson and the gifts, but at least he had profited from his spendthrift days, and the regret no longer seemed so purposeless.

Accept Responsibility, Make Amends

The principle of accepting responsibility for your wrongs and mistakes and then making amends for them is a continuing application of Step Five ("Making Amends"). To maintain a regret-free life, apply this principle of accepting responsibility and making amends *whenever you realize that you have erred or wronged somebody.* Prompt apologies and reparations prevent a regret from festering and remaining with you.

Jack, for example, discovered the salutary effect of making amends when he acknowledged responsibility for his emotional outburst at the office. Someone had accused him of making an error in the financial statements, which, as it turned out, was true. Jack made amends within the hour for both his mistake, which he acknowledged, and his emotional outburst, which he regretted. The offended parties had not expected his quick apology—even though they thought they deserved it—and their anger melted into respect. Even so, Jack made the amend for himself to stay regret-free, not for them.

In a larger sense, the principle of accepting responsibility means accepting responsibility for your life as a whole and for making it the best you can regardless of your circumstances. When your regrets and unrealistic thought patterns keep you focused on what might have been, they deprive you of the true playing field of power: the present. Other than through your reparations, you cannot change the past. You can, however, change the present. By living in your regrets, you give up the power of the present, trading it for the powerlessness of the past. Those who say, "I am unhappy with my life today because of what happened to me then" are indulging a fantasy. They are unhappy today because of how they react to the events of today—not to the events of the past—no matter how tragic the past events were. If they accepted that reality, however, they would have to do something about their outlook or their present circumstances.

At first it is difficult to believe how much power we have to change the way we see ourselves, our situation, and the world with which we interact. That power gives us a major role in determining the quality of our present lives as well as the future into which the present will evolve. The perceptions and beliefs we hold about life will determine how we interpret the events of life, whether past or present. To prove that to yourself, read the extraordinary book *Man's Search for Meaning,* by Viktor Frankl. It is the autobiographical account of a Jewish psychiatrist imprisoned in a Nazi death camp who found purpose and meaning despite horrific, virtually unimaginable circumstances. In his book, Frankl writes of what he had learned about surviving day to day under such conditions. "We may not be able to change our fate," he writes, "but by the defiant power of the human spirit, we can change our attitude." That change in attitude saved his life.

Man's Search for Meaning is a powerful book that makes clear the two simple alternatives that life offers when things are not going our way: change the things we can change or accept the things we cannot change. When we accept what we cannot change, however, we do in fact change something: our attitude. A change in attitude alters our perception of events and thus our reaction to them. It changes us. Of course, such attitudinal changes are not necessarily easy to make, but they are immensely rewarding. If you are unhappy today, it is because you are refusing to change something you can change (usually your attitude, perceptions, or actions) while trying insistently to change something you cannot change (usually other people, events, or situations beyond your control).

The big lie of regrets is that the past is the source of our unhappiness. It isn't. The source of our unhappiness is how we deal with the present. If we are unhappy, it is not because we are victims of the past. It is because we are victims of ourselves.

Stay Grateful

Cultivating gratitude increases humility and paves the way for spiritual growth. Being grateful is a way of interacting with the world that must be nourished. A sense of gratitude is strengthened by practice. Make a list of the things for which you are grateful, large and small, especially when you are tempted to return to old regrets. Making a mental gratitude list as part of your daily prayers or a written list when difficulties arise will lessen your anxieties and encourage your spirit. Engage in "good remembering," recalling the good that came from your regrets, the gifts of the new path they set you on, and the blessings of your present life. Gratitude genuinely held and often acknowledged is a potent means of avoiding regrets and overcoming sadness and fear. New research published in the *Journal of Personality and Social Psychology* indicates that people who make a daily list of the things for which they are grateful enjoy better mental health, exercise more, sleep better, and care more about other people.

A sense of gratitude is reassuring. It reminds us that we are not alone in the world and that our higher power is involved with us. Gratitude allows us to recognize that the changes taking place in us are greater than our own capabilities would have allowed, and it acknowledges the lessons and gifts we've been offered through the fortunes and misfortunes of our lives. Gratitude leads us to develop trust in a divine order and purpose, understanding that we cannot fully fathom it at the present time. As we acknowledge the blessing in our lives, we come to terms with the past and its pain, with the present and its mysteries, and with the future and its possibilities. Life in all its potentiality opens up to us.

Practice Humility

Some degree of humility is essential to spiritual growth and psychological development. Humility is a realistic assessment of your role in the world and a recognition of your limitations, neither overestimating your power and responsibility nor underestimating them. Humility allows you to see your own imperfections and to accept the limitations of others, to make mistakes, and to forgive mistakes. It also allows you to appreciate your genuine accomplishments and achievements.

Spiritually, humility is the effort to align your will with your higher power's will for you. Such an alignment is ego-deflating, of course, and determining God's will is no easy task, either. Nonetheless, a recognition that you are not the center of the world around you, that you may not know as much as you think, and that some principles are more important than your desires are major contributors to the development and maintenance of humility.

There are many expressions of humility and many ways to achieve and practice it. Some of the actions you can take to increase your humility are:

- Pray each day to your higher power, asking for knowledge of your higher power's will for you.
- Apply spiritual and psychological tools and principles regularly.
- Listen deeply to what other people say, as if every conversation with another person were a prayer between the two of you.
- Strive for tolerance, compassion, and understanding in your dealings with others and yourself. Judge people less.
- Forgive others quickly, completely, and generously. Forgive yourself in the same way.
- Admit mistakes and make quick amends for them.
- Accept help from others when it is offered and needed.
- Ask for help when it is needed but not offered.
- Find ways to serve.
- Thank your higher power regularly for all you have been given in your life.

Serve Others

The habit of serving others is both the result of humility and a means of strengthening humility. But service to others is also a source of satisfaction and a way out of a preoccupation with yourself and your troubles. When you are helping someone in need, it is hard to be overly concerned about yourself. From the many ways to serve, choose those that capitalize on your unique gifts. Time, talent, and treasure are the traditional ways of giving, but time and talent are more effective in maintaining gratitude and humility than gifts of money alone. Any form of service that keeps your life in perspective is worthwhile. But a form of service that puts to use the lessons and gifts of your regrets will be particularly beneficial to you and to others.

Opportunities for such service abound. For example, an alcoholic in recovery can help other alcoholics achieve sobriety. An abused spouse can offer counsel to those who seek to leave their own abusive relationships. A family with a teenager lost to suicide can commit itself to educating others about the prevalence and prevention of adolescent suicide. A person who dropped out of school can devote time to encouraging youngsters to stay in school. Many of the lessons and gifts we have received from our regrets can also be passed on in the course of being good parents and friends.

Forgive Yourself and Others

Now that you have forgiven yourself and others for your regrets, you know that you can continue to forgive whenever the need arises. Like humility, service, and gratitude, forgiveness is an essential quality of the regret-free life. Forgive others for real wrongs committed against you and for imagined wrongs, such as not being the people you want them to be. Forgive them so that you can enjoy your own life.

Forgive yourself for daily mistakes, misjudgments, and failures even as you try to correct them. Perfection is not the goal, and you do not have to judge yourself by its unrealistic standards. Develop tolerance, patience, and compassion for yourself just as you are developing it for others. Test your progress by forgiving regularly. Avoid creating or holding resentments, which will poison the gardens of your life.

Accept Others, Accept Life

The more you grow spiritually, the more accepting you will become of other people and of life's events over which you have no control. The Serenity Prayer sets the standard: "God, grant me the serenity to accept the things I cannot change, courage to change the things I can, and the wisdom to know the difference." Acceptance of what you cannot change is a key to contentment. Acceptance frees you from resentments and allows you to face the difficulties of life with equanimity and seasoned faith. You will be less judgmental and more tolerant of people and things you do not understand or with which you disagree. You will be less easily offended and quicker to forgive, less frequently aroused to anger, and more appreciative of this extraordinary world in which we live. Acceptance is an activity as well as a state of being. It requires hard work to acquire and to apply. But the payoff is high. Accepting what you cannot change is a powerful way to shape your experiences in the world and, when necessary, to triumph over them.

Reject Old Regrets

Never entertain an old regret. Not for a minute, not for a second. Do not indulge it. Do not return to its seductive pleasures or destructive effects for any reason once you have let it go through the Ten Steps. Refuse to rekindle its resentments, to suffer old bouts of self-pity, or to engage in old episodes of blaming. Use thought analysis and the other spiritual and psychological tools to keep you out of its pain and anger.

Staying regret-free does not mean that you can't remember and apply the lessons and gifts of your regrets, however. You can. But to remember a regret, apply its lessons, or use its gifts is not the same as falling back into the regret, reliving the past it represents, blaming yourself, or indulging "if only" fantasies of what might have been.

Just as you do not entertain old regrets that pop into your mind, do not entertain old regrets that others try to rekindle in you. In letting go of your regrets, you have completed a remarkable journey. Your regrets are now in the past where they belong, because you have let them go. But others may not have let them go, may not be willing to let them go, or may not want *you* to let them go. For many reasons, people may try to convince you to take back your old regrets. They may do so because they enjoy inflicting pain, because they want to remind you that they were "right," because they enjoy arguments, because they want to punish you, because they want a fellow victim, because they resent your progress, because they want to continue as martyrs, because it keeps them from having to look at their own regrets, because, because, because . . . The reason doesn't matter.

When someone tries to remind you of your regrets, whether as victim, perpetrator, observer, or interested party, your answer to them is always a version of the same theme: "I've let go of that regret." You may want to expand on that idea with something like, "If you are genuinely interested in letting go of your regrets, I'll be happy to share my experience with you so that you can let go of yours. But I won't discuss the old regret again." Those who wish you well will respect your request and act accordingly. They will drop the regret. Those who are genuinely seeking your help will ask you how you let go of the regret. If they do, that is an opportunity to share how you did it and, perhaps, to help them let go of theirs.

Some people, however, do not want you to let go of your regrets because they have a substantial investment in them. If they find that you have let them go, they will try to persuade you to resurrect them. Resist. Regardless of their words, decline the bait. Refuse to go back to the regret, politely if you can, impolitely if you must. Regardless of how insistent or aggressive you have to be, it is imperative that you keep yourself regret-free and solidly in the present. You have a right to protect yourself and your happiness from those who wish you ill or simply act out of ignorance. You must not allow yourself to be talked back into the shame and guilt you have left behind.

To those who stubbornly return to your regrets and try to involve you in them, respond with something like, "I'm sorry that old regret is still a problem for you. I've let it go." Or give them a copy of *No Regrets* inscribed, "You can let the regret go, too." You need not allow someone to abuse you emotionally just as you would not allow someone to abuse you physically. With such people, you have to be aggressive in protecting yourself, which is not only your right, but your responsibility.

Let Go of New Regrets

New regrets will inevitably arise. Life is like that. You will make mistakes, other people will make mistakes, circumstances will not be to your liking, things will happen. Out of these events, you may develop new regrets. Some of these regrets will be warranted. You should regret your actions when you do something wrong. You can't help but regret other people's actions when they hurt you. But you do not have to harbor the regrets. You can let them go. You have learned how to let go of your regrets using the Ten Steps. You can protect yourself from holding onto new regrets by applying the Ten Steps before those new regrets fester. Protecting yourself in this way is your daily responsibility.

Live Resolutely in the Present

Those who live in the present are free of regrets, because regrets belong to the past. One of the malignant features of all regrets is that they siphon the present out of us, making us a victim or perpetrator again and returning us to a time when we were unhappy. When we regret, we leave the present where we can change our lives to visit the past where we can change nothing. The past is remembered, but only the present is lived. When we live one day at a time—borrowing neither from the past nor the future—we remain focused on the events and people of the present moment with all the gifts and love and wonder they have to offer.

Just as you refuse to indulge old regrets about the past, refuse to indulge fears about the future, which are equally corrosive. Old regrets and future fears both belong to fantasy worlds. Neither exists. Only the present is real. Each day begins that present anew. So does each hour. You are entitled to carry over whatever you want from the day before, the year before, or the decade before. You can wallow in your regrets, in what was lost or never was. But there is another alternative: seize the present moment and live it to the fullest.

All of these options to use or squander the gifts of the present moment are yours, because life is yours to live as you choose. You cannot control life's events or other people, but you can control yourself. You can control how you perceive the world and how you respond to it. That control is absolute, and it is all you need. Exercising that control wisely on life's journey is the road less traveled. And that makes all the difference.

With the completion of the Tenth Step, your journey of letting go of your regrets is complete. If you think through what you have accomplished, you will see it for the remarkable achievement it is. Whether your regrets spanned months, years, or decades, they have lost their power to hurt you, to stain your present life, and to erode the quality of your days. Whatever bound you to those regrets and to the past they represent has been cut. You are free to live and free to claim the present moment, unblemished by shadows of the past.

The journey that Step Ten launched will take you to many unexpected destinations of the mind and heart. Your new journey holds the promise of unexplored territories filled with life-fulfilling experiences of every kind, already awaiting your arrival. Some will bring exquisite joy and some exquisite sadness, but regardless of what the future holds on the broad highways and the quiet cul de sacs of your travels, you will have nothing to regret.

Yet wherever you travel, you will not be far from home. Home is always the present moment, where life's joys are experienced and its richest treasures are found. You may visit the future in anticipation, or you may drop by the past for the quick pleasure of happy memories, but your life belongs to the present. Your heart belongs to the present. It is only in the present that life continues to unfold, that human interaction is possible, and that you are really alive. This is the home that calls you.

The Ten Steps, especially the tenth step, will keep you living in the present for the whole of life's journey. The spiritual tools and principles will guide you in making decisions at every fork in the road, even the forks you had not anticipated and those you would rather not have had to take. The power of the steps, their tools, and principles is such that you can travel with confidence, even in the midst of uncertainty, losing the pain of regrets even as the past that contains them slips away. In place of regretting, you will rediscover the wonder of the world as young children experience it—a world of fascination, surprise, and love. Neither beholden to the past nor mortgaged to the future, you will discover in the eternity of the present moment the priceless gift of *being*.

This is the road of the present, the road less traveled, the road that makes all the difference.

Welcome back to the present. Welcome home.

Appendix A

RECOMMENDED READING

Each of the following books offers additional insight into some aspect of the process of letting go of regrets and is well worth reading.

Fanning, Patrick. *Visualization for Change.* Oakland, Calif.: New Harbinger Publications, 1994.

A very thorough treatment of creative visualization, including its history, basic practices, and applications. The book covers a variety of problems and self-improvement opportunities to which creative visualization can be applied, such as weight control, goal achievement, improved sports performance, healing, stress reduction, insomnia, shyness, and depression, among others. You will have a thorough understanding of creative visualization and how to do it after reading this book.

Frankl, Viktor E. *Man's Search for Meaning.* New York: Washington Square Press, 1997.

This remarkable autobiography recounts the story of a Jewish psychiatrist imprisoned during World War II in a Nazi concentration camp. It recounts not only how Dr. Frankl survived the camp but how he came to find meaning in his experience there. The book is an essential read for anyone who wants to understand the power of the human mind to shape the meaning of experience. It is also profoundly inspiring. The book has sold over 2.5 million copies.

Gawain, Shakti. *Creative Visualization*. New York: Bantam Books, 1982.

A simple guidebook to creative visualization written with tenderness and full of examples to guide you through the process. This book has been an international best-seller. It is shorter and more personal than *Visualization for Change*, but the two books complement each other well.

Nelson, Mariah Burton. *The Unburdened Heart*. New York: Harper-Collins, 2000.

This autobiographical book will be very helpful to readers having trouble forgiving those who have hurt them. It recounts the story of a woman who was molested as a teenager by one of her high school teachers and of her struggle to forgive him. Beautifully and engagingly written, it is a testament to the power of forgiveness to heal and to change the lives of those who forgive. The book includes a description of the process Ms. Nelson developed for forgiving others as a means of finding lasting peace.

Peck, M. Scott. *The Road Less Traveled*. New York: Touchstone, 1978.

One of the most remarkable self-help books ever written (ten years on the *New York Times* best-seller list), this gift from Dr. Peck to all of us explains how to confront, embrace, and use the difficulties that life inevitably hands us. It also contains an important discussion on the meaning of love and how we can become more loving as individuals and more receptive to love from others. Finally, it explores the necessity of spiritual growth as well as psychological growth for those who want to experience life at its richest. The book has helped untold numbers of people improve the quality of their lives, and it remains as relevant today as it was the year it was published.

Appendix B

SUMMARY OF THE TEN-STEP ACTION LISTS

This appendix contains a summary of the Action Lists for each of the Ten Steps:

Step One: Listing Regrets
1. Name of the regret
2. Description of the regret
3. Category of the regret
4. Feelings about the regret
5. "If onlys"

Step Two: Examining Regrets
1. Your role in creating the regret
2. Those you hurt in the regret
3. Those you blame for the regret
4. Consequences of holding onto the regret

Step Three: Changing Toxic Thought Patterns
1. Analyze each regret for toxic thought patterns that support it
2. Use thought analysis to counter the toxic thoughts that support the regret

Step Four: Grieving Losses
   1. Describe the losses of your regrets
   2. Grieve your losses

Step Five: Making Amends
   1. Determine the appropriate amends for the request
   2. Make the apology and reparations
   3. Change the harmful behavior

Step Six: Identifying Lessons and Gifts
   1. Identify the lessons of each regret
   2. Identify the gifts of each regret
   3. Apply the lessons and gifts for the benefit of ourselves
   4. Apply the lessons and gifts for the benefit of others

Step Seven: Developing Compassion
   1. Assess your capacities at the time of the regret
   2. Identify what you did right
   3. Apply the spiritual and psychological tools

Step Eight: Forgiving Others
   1. List the people to forgive
   2. Reasons your forgiveness is needed
   3. Benefits of forgiving
   4. Reasons for not forgiving
   5. The act of forgiveness

Step Nine: Forgiving Ourselves
   1. Why I need to forgive myself
   2. Reasons to forgive myself
   3. Reasons for not forgiving myself
   4. Overcoming resistance to forgiving myself

5. The act of forgiving myself
6. Letting go of your regrets

Step Ten: Living Free of Regret
1. Apply the spiritual and psychological tools and principles to daily life

Appendix C

QUICK REFERENCE: TOOLS, PRINCIPLES, AND TOXIC THOUGHT PATTERNS

This is a quick reference guide to which you can turn while working the Ten Steps. It will also be handy in the future as you continue working Step Ten. It summarizes:

- The Ten Steps to Letting Go of Regret
- Spiritual and Psychological Tools
- Spiritual and Psychological Principles
- Toxic Thought Patterns

The Ten Steps to Letting Go of Regret

1. Listing Regrets
2. Examining Regrets
3. Changing Toxic Thought Patterns
4. Grieving Losses
5. Making Amends
6. Identifying Lessons and Gifts
7. Developing Compassion
8. Forgiving Others

9. Forgiving Ourselves
10. Living Free of Regret

Spiritual and Psychological Tools (chapter 3)

1. *Thought analysis:* used to analyze your regrets, the events associated with them, the feelings you have about them, and the way in which you think about them; to change the way you think and feel about your regrets.
2. *Journaling:* used to catalogue and analyze your regrets, to clarify your thoughts, and to express your feelings.
3. *Prayer:* used to gain the insight, courage, discipline, strength, and other resources you need to work each step.
4. *Sharing with others:* used to gain insight and emotional support from others in working the steps.
5. *Affirmations:* used to overcome resistance and to facilitate working the steps.
6. *Creative visualization:* used to overcome resistance and to facilitate working the steps.

Toxic Thought Patterns (chapter 6)

1. Perfectionism
2. Exaggerated control
3. Foreseeing the future
4. Knowing what others are thinking
5. Personalizing events
6. Incomplete comparisons
7. Undeserved guilt
8. Reimagining the past
9. Extreme thinking
10. Using regrets as justification for inaction

Spiritual and Psychological Principles (chapter 13)

1. Apply the lessons and gifts of your regrets.
2. Accept responsibility, make amends.
3. Stay grateful.
4. Practice humility.
5. Serve others.
6. Forgive yourself and others.
7. Accept others, accept life.
8. Reject old regrets.
9. Let go of new regrets.
10. Live resolutely in the present.

INDEX

victim role, 96–97
visualization, creative
  as spiritual and
    psychological tool, 38,
    52–59
  in Step Eight, 168
  in Step Five, 116
  in Step Four, 105
  in Step Nine, 181
  in Step One, 66

  in Step Seven, 149
  in Step Six, 141
  in Step Ten, 190–191
  in Step Two, 74
  Visualization for Change (Fanning),
    53–54

willingness, 4, 30, 31, 32
wisdom, 133–134
writing. *See* journaling

Hamilton Beazley, Ph.D., is scholar-in-residence at St. Edward's University, Austin, Texas, and a former associate professor in the Department of Psychology at The George Washington University, Washington, D.C. He received his B.A. degree in psychology from Yale University and his Ph.D. in organizational behavior from The George Washington University. The supporting field of his doctoral studies was contemporary spirituality. He is a member of the American Psychological Association.

Before his academic career, Dr. Beazley served in a variety of executive positions. He is the former president of the National Council on Alcoholism and Drug Dependence, New York City, a former member of the Executive Committee of the Division on Addictions of the Harvard Medical School, and a member of the Board of Trustees of the Educational Advancement Foundation.

NoRegrets.org is the official website for *No Regrets.*

Made in the USA
Lexington, KY
24 March 2011